TAPESTRY

REAL
CONTEXTS

TAPESTRY

The **Tapestry** program of language
materials is based on the concepts
presented in *The Tapestry of
Language Learning: The Individual
in the Communicative Classroom* by
Robin C. Scarcella &
Rebecca L. Oxford.

Each title in this program focuses on:

Individual learner strategies and
instruction

The relatedness of skills

Ongoing self-assessment

Authentic material as input

Theme-based learning linked to task-
based instruction

Attention to all aspects of
communicative competence

REAL CONTEXTS

Neil J. Anderson

Heinle & Heinle Publishers
An International Thomson
  Publishing Company
Boston, Massachusetts, 02116, USA

The publication of *Real Contexts* was directed by the members of the Heinle & Heinle Global Innovations Publishing Team:

David C. Lee, Editorial Director
John F. McHugh, Market Development Director
Lisa J. McLaughlin, Senior Production Services Coordinator

Also participating in the publication of this program were:

Director of Production: Elizabeth Holthaus
Publisher: Stanley J. Galek
Senior Assistant Editor: Kenneth Mattsson
Production Editor: Maryellen Eschmann Killeen
Manufacturing Coordinator: Mary Beth Hennebury
Full Service Project Manager/Compositor: PC&F, Inc.
Art: Dave Blanchette and PC&F, Inc.
Interior Design: Maureen Lauran
Cover Design: Maureen Lauran
Photo/Video Specialist: Jonathan Stark

Manufactured in the United States of America

ISBN: 0-8384-4706-6

Heinle & Heinle Publishers is an International Thomson Publishing Company.

10 9 8 7 6 5 4 3 2

To Kathy, Cameron, Todd,
Amy, Ryan, and Douglas:
the people in my real context!

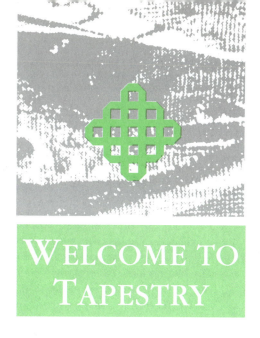

WELCOME TO TAPESTRY

*E*nter the world of Tapestry! Language learning can be seen as an ever-developing tapestry woven with many threads and colors. The elements of the tapestry are related to different language skills like listening and speaking, reading and writing; the characteristics of the teachers; the desires, needs, and backgrounds of the students; and the general second language development process. When all these elements are working together harmoniously, the result is a colorful, continuously growing tapestry of language competence of which the student and the teacher can be proud.

This volume is part of the Tapestry Program for students of English as a second language (ESL) at levels from beginning to "bridge" (which follows the advanced level and prepares students to enter regular postsecondary programs along with native English speakers). Upper level materials in the Tapestry Program are also appropriate for developmental English courses—especially reading and composition courses. Tapestry levels include:

Beginning	Advanced
Low Intermediate	High Advanced
High Intermediate	Bridge

Because the Tapestry Program provides a unified theoretical and pedagogical foundation for all its components, you can optimally use all the Tapestry student books in a coordinated fashion as an entire curriculum of materials. (They will be published from 1993 to 1996 with further editions likely thereafter.) Alternatively, you can decide to use just certain Tapestry volumes, depending on your specific needs.

Tapestry is primarily designed for ESL students at postsecondary institutions in North America. Some want to learn ESL for academic or career advancement, others for social and personal reasons. Tapestry builds directly on all these motivations. Tapestry stimulates learners to do their best. It enables learners to use English naturally and to develop fluency as well as accuracy.

Tapestry Principles

The following principles underlie the instruction provided in all of the components of the Tapestry Program.

EMPOWERING LEARNERS

Language learners in Tapestry classrooms are active and increasingly responsible for developing their English language skills and related cultural abilities. This self direction leads to better, more rapid learning. Some cultures virtually train their students to be passive in the classroom, but Tapestry weans them from passivity by providing exceptionally high interest materials, colorful and motivating activities, personalized self-reflection tasks, peer tutoring and other forms of cooperative learning, and powerful learning strategies to boost self direction in learning.

The empowerment of learners creates refreshing new roles for teachers, too. The teacher serves as facilitator, co-communicator, diagnostician, guide, and helper. Teachers are set free to be more creative at the same time their students become more autonomous learners.

HELPING STUDENTS IMPROVE THEIR LEARNING STRATEGIES

Learning strategies are the behaviors or steps an individual uses to enhance his or her learning. Examples are taking notes, practicing, finding a conversation partner, analyzing words, using background knowledge, and controlling anxiety. Hundreds of such strategies have been identified. Successful language learners use language learning strategies that are most effective for them given their particular learning style, and they put them together smoothly to fit the needs of a given language task. On the other hand, the learning strategies of less successful learners are a desperate grab-bag of ill-matched techniques.

All learners need to know a wide range of learning strategies. All learners need systematic practice in choosing and applying strategies that are relevant for various learning needs. Tapestry is one of the only ESL programs that overtly weaves a comprehensive set of learning strategies into language activities in all its volumes. These learning strategies are arranged in eight broad categories throughout the Tapestry books:

Forming Concepts
Personalizing
Remembering New Material
Managing Your Learning
Understanding and Using Emotions
Overcoming Limitations
Testing Hypotheses
Learning with Others

The most useful strategies are sometimes repeated and flagged with a note, "It Works! Learning Strategy . . ." to remind students to use a learning strategy they have already encountered. This recycling reinforces the value of learning strategies and provides greater practice.

RECOGNIZING AND HANDLING LEARNING STYLES EFFECTIVELY

Learners have different learning styles (for instance, visual, auditory, hands-on; reflective, impulsive; analytic, global; extroverted, introverted; closure-oriented, open). Particularly in an ESL setting, where students come from vastly different cultural backgrounds, learning styles differences abound and can cause "style conflicts."

Unlike most language instruction materials, Tapestry provides exciting activities specifically tailored to the needs of students with a large range of learning styles. You can use any Tapestry volume with the confidence that the activities and materials are intentionally geared for many different styles. Insights from the latest educational and psychological research undergird this style-nourishing variety.

OFFERING AUTHENTIC, MEANINGFUL COMMUNICATION

Students need to encounter language that provides authentic, meaningful communication. They must be involved in real-life communication tasks that cause them to *want* and *need* to read, write, speak, and listen to English. Moreover, the tasks—to be most effective—must be arranged around themes relevant to learners.

Themes like family relationships, survival in the educational system, personal health, friendships in a new country, political changes, and protection of the environment are all valuable to ESL learners. Tapestry focuses on topics like these. In every Tapestry volume, you will see specific content drawn from very broad areas such as home life, science and technology, business, humanities, social sciences, global issues, and multiculturalism. All the themes are real and important, and they are fashioned into language tasks that students enjoy.

At the advanced level, Tapestry also includes special books each focused on a single broad theme. For instance, there are two books on business English, two on English for science and technology, and two on academic communication and study skills.

UNDERSTANDING AND VALUING DIFFERENT CULTURES

Many ESL books and programs focus completely on the "new" culture, that is, the culture which the students are entering. The implicit message is that ESL students should just learn about this target culture, and there is no need to understand their own culture better or to find out about the cultures of their international classmates. To some ESL students, this makes them feel their own culture is not valued in the new country.

Tapestry is designed to provide a clear and understandable entry into North American culture. Nevertheless, the Tapestry Program values *all* the cultures found in the ESL classroom. Tapestry students have constant opportunities to become "culturally fluent" in North American culture while they are learning English, but they also have the chance to think about the cultures of their classmates and even understand their home culture from different perspectives.

INTEGRATING THE LANGUAGE SKILLS

Communication in a language is not restricted to one skill or another. ESL students are typically expected to learn (to a greater or lesser degree) all four language skills: reading, writing, speaking, and listening. They are also expected to develop strong grammatical competence, as well as becoming socioculturally sensitive and knowing what to do when they encounter a "language barrier."

Research shows that multi-skill learning is more effective than isolated-skill learning, because related activities in several skills provide reinforcement and refresh the learner's memory. Therefore, Tapestry integrates all the skills. A given Tapestry volume might highlight one skill, such as reading, but all other skills are also included to support and strengthen overall language development.

However, many intensive ESL programs are divided into classes labeled according to one skill (Reading Comprehension Class) or at most two skills (Listening/Speaking Class or Oral Communication Class). The volumes in the Tapestry Program can easily be used to fit this traditional format, because each volume clearly identifies its highlighted or central skill(s).

Grammar is interwoven into all Tapestry volumes. However, there is also a separate reference book for students, *The Tapestry Grammar,* and a Grammar Strand composed of grammar "work-out" books at each of the levels in the Tapestry Program.

Other Features of the Tapestry Program

PILOT SITES

It is not enough to provide volumes full of appealing tasks and beautiful pictures. Users deserve to know that the materials have been pilot-tested. In many ESL series, pilot testing takes place at only a few sites or even just in the classroom of the author. In contrast, Heinle & Heinle Publishers have developed a network of Tapestry Pilot Test Sites throughout North America. At this time, there are approximately 40 such sites, although the number grows weekly. These sites try out the materials and provide suggestions for revisions. They are all actively engaged in making Tapestry the best program possible.

AN OVERALL GUIDEBOOK

To offer coherence to the entire Tapestry Program and especially to offer support for teachers who want to understand the principles and practice of Tapestry, we have written a book entitled, *The Tapestry of Language Learning. The Individual in the Communicative Classroom* (Scarcella and Oxford, published in 1992 by Heinle & Heinle).

A Last Word

We are pleased to welcome you to Tapestry! We use the Tapestry principles every day, and we hope these principles—and all the books in the Tapestry Program—provide you the same strength, confidence, and joy that they give us. We look forward to comments from both teachers and students who use any part of the Tapestry Program.

Rebecca L. Oxford
University of Alabama
Tuscaloosa, Alabama

Robin C. Scarcella
University of California at Irvine
Irvine, California

PREFACE

*T*he primary goal of *Real Contexts* is to provide opportunities in which low-intermediate readers can develop and improve their reading skills, reading strategies, and reading rate. The text is designed for 40–50 instructional hours. In programs of shorter duration the teacher can select which chapters to read with the class. An important thing to be aware of in terms of reading rate development is that it is difficult to see significant increases in one's reading rate over a short period of time. The longer students can work on their reading rate the more progress they will see.

Intended Audience

The intended audience for this textbook is nonnative speakers of English who are studying in the United States. It is assumed that these students are young adults interested in attending a university in the United States. The intended audience is at the low-intermediate level of language proficiency with approximately a 1,000-word recognition vocabulary.

Features of *Real Contexts*

Real Contexts is based upon the theoretical and pedagogical principles of ACTIVE reading outlined by Anderson (1992) which suggest that reading materials should include activities that allow teachers to:

> **A**ctivate prior knowledge
> **C**ultivate vocabulary
> **T**each for comprehension
> **I**ncrease reading rate
> **V**erify reading strategies
> **E**valuate progress

Each chapter in *Real Contexts* provides reading opportunities in each of these areas.

PRIMARY FEATURES

- The first chapter discusses reading rate and reading comprehension and provides a student information sheet that examines the reading habits and interests of the students.
- Several readings in eight additional thematically-organized chapters provide extended practice in the development of reading skills, reading strategies, as well as reading rate.
- A *personalized* approach to each of the chapters. The text seeks to point out to the reader how each topic is relevant to his or her personal life.
- Explicit reading rate development activities are included with each reading passage. Four primary-rate exercises are implemented throughout the text: rate buildup reading, repeated reading, class-paced reading, and self-paced reading. These development activities are not designed to get readers to read thousands of words per minute but to increase their reading rate to a threshold rate level of approximately 200 words-per-minute.
- *Real Contexts* offers nine 1,000-word timed readings that measure reading rate as well as assess reading comprehension. Students record their reading rate and comprehension scores on a chart included in the appendix. These chapter reading passages can be used to evaluate reading rate and comprehension growth throughout the course.
- *Real Contexts* also provides an integration of all language skills: listening, speaking, and writing, as well as development of reading skills.

It is my hope that *Real Contexts* will help you improve your English reading skills so that you are more successful in your real contexts!

Acknowledgments

A special expression of gratitude is extended to the ESL learners in my classes over the past 15 years who have helped me think through the ideas and activities that are contained in *Real Contexts*. In a very real sense, the contexts of each chapter have emerged from discussions with learners in the classroom.

Very helpful suggestions have been provided by Rebecca L. Oxford, Robin Scarcella, David Lee, Ken Mattsson from Heinle & Heinle and other reviewers: Mary Azawi, William Rainey Harper College; Doborah Busch, Delaware County Community College; Mary Hebert, University of California at Davis; Kathy Hitchcox, International English Institute; Patrick Oglesby, Duke University; Nancy Pfingstag, University of North Carolina at Charlotte; Merce Pujol, Hostos Community College, and Norman Yoshida, Lewis and Clark College. Their suggestions have helped me move outside my own context to include ideas and activities that can be of benefit to learners in the classroom. I also express thanks to my colleagues in the Department of Linguistics at Ohio University. The continued support of my Chair, Richard McGinn is greatly appreciated.

My hope is that each learner who uses this text will have a real purpose for language learning and that learning will be facilitated through the reading passages and activities contained here.

Neil J. Anderson
Ohio University, Athens, OH

CONTENTS

Your Background: What Are Your Real Contexts?

In this first chapter, you will learn about your learning contexts and about the way you learn languages. You will complete three questionnaires that will help you learn about your reading preferences, reading rate, language learning strategies, and language learning style. Answer the following questions about your reading habits and background for your teacher.

Student Information Sheet

Name _____

Name you would like to be called in class _____

Home city and country _____

Native language _____

Local address _____

Local telephone number _____

Date of birth _____

How many years did you study English in your home country?_____

Have you studied English in the United States?   yes   no

    Where? _____

    When? _____

Have you studied English in other countries?   yes   no

    Where? _____

    When? _____

Do you plan to study at a university in the United States?   yes   no

    Where? _____

    When? _____

What is your intended major field of study? _____

Do you enjoy reading in your native language?   yes   no

How long do you read daily (on an average) in your native language?

_____

What types of material do you read in your native language?

_____

Do you enjoy reading in English?   yes   no

How long do you read daily (on an average) in English? _____

What types of material do you read in English? _____

_____

List ten things you consider strengths about your reading.

   1. _____

   2. _____

   3. _____

   4. _____

   5. _____

   6. _____

   7. _____

   8. _____

   9. _____

 10. _____

List ten things you would like to improve in your reading.

   1. _____

   2. _____

   3. _____

   4. _____

   5. _____

   6. _____

   7. _____

   8. _____

   9. _____

 10. _____

What is the title of your favorite book? _____

What is your favorite movie? _____

What is your favorite type of music? _____

What are some of your hobbies? _____

_____

_____

What do you hope to learn in this reading class? _____

_____

_____

Write an introductory paragraph about yourself. Include any information you would like others to know about you.

_____

_____

_____

_____

_____

_____

_____

_____

_____

_____

_____

Silently read the following introductory passage to help you become familiar with how *Real Contexts* is organized. Your teacher will time your reading to get an initial assessment of your reading rate. After reading, look up at your teacher and write down the time shown on the card. The purpose of this reading is to find out how many words per minute you can read. Do not stop to look up unknown vocabulary or to look at the appendices. Your goal is to read this section without stopping to learn how fast you currently read.

PRINCIPLES OF ACTIVE READING

Reading is an essential skill for students who desire to attend an American university. With strengthened reading skills, you will make greater progress in developing all
5 aspects of language learning, including listening, speaking, and writing.

Real Contexts applies principles of ACTIVE reading to help you develop strong reading skills. The six principles of ACTIVE
10 reading are:
- Activate prior knowledge
- Cultivate vocabulary
- Teach for comprehension
- Increase reading rate
15 - Verify reading strategies
- Evaluate progress

The ACTIVE reading framework provides the organization for *Real Contexts* and is a way for the teacher to help you
20 improve your reading skills.

You probably already know that vocabulary and comprehension are important to reading. Did you know that the experiences you have had in life also
25 are important to reading? Your prior knowledge or experience helps you to understand what you read. These experiences cause you to think about what you are reading so you can judge what
30 is true and what is not true. When you read something that you already know something about it is easier for you to read fast and to understand. When we read something new we think about how it is related to
35 something we already know. In that way we are able to understand and remember what we read. As you begin each reading in *Real Contexts* you will be able to think about what you already know about the topic.

40 Each chapter in *Real Contexts* has a timed reading passage of approximately 1,000 words followed by ten multiple-choice comprehension questions. The purpose of these passages is to give you focused practice

45 on improving your reading rate. When we say "improving your reading rate," we do not mean that you should read hundreds of words per minute, but that you should read at a reasonable rate for a university student.
50 An appropriate reading rate for university students is approximately 200 words per minute. Two charts in the appendices (Appendix B and Appendix C) will be used to help you keep track of your reading rate
55 and your reading comprehension after completing the timed readings in each chapter. These charts will be helpful as you set goals to improve your reading rate.

Teaching reading strategies and helping
60 you to be aware of your reading strategies is an important part of *Real Contexts*. Throughout the text, various reading strategies are highlighted. Be aware of what you do as you read. This will help make you
65 a better reader. Not all readers use the same strategies. Some strategies may be easy for you to use, others may be difficult. You should pay attention to what works for you and try new strategies even though they may
70 be difficult at first. You can improve your reading as you experiment with new reading strategies.

Evaluating your success as a reader comes in many forms. You should pay close
75 attention as you read and monitor your comprehension. When you don't understand what you are reading, what do you do? Are you already aware of some of your strengths as a reader? Are you aware of your
80 weaknesses as a reader? When you miss a comprehension question on a test, why have you missed it? These are all important questions to consider. *Real Contexts* will give you many chances to evaluate your
85 reading progress. It is difficult to evaluate progress over a short period of time. You may not see much progress after one or two weeks, but after nine or ten weeks you

should be able to see where you are getting
90 better.

One way to help you improve your reading is to keep a reading log. A reading log is a record of what you read. One purpose of a reading log is to help you keep
95 a record of how much reading you do every day. Also, good readers read many different kinds of texts, so the log will help you keep track of the different kinds of text you read each day. Your teacher may ask you to keep
100 a reading log and submit it on a weekly basis. Some teachers may ask you to read for 30 minutes every day outside of class and to write in your log the title of what you read and for how long. Other teachers may ask
105 you to write a short description of what you read. Some may ask you to react to what you have read. Also, by sharing with others what we are reading we can learn from each other. A sample reading log that you can use
110 to keep track of what you read outside of class is found in Appendix A.

Why do people read? This question is important to success in reading. You should always ask yourself why you are
115 reading and what you hope to learn as you read. Two broad, general reasons for reading can be reading for information and reading for pleasure. When you read for information you read the text with the goal
120 of being able to get new information or to increase your learning. When you read for pleasure you read to relax and enjoy what you are reading. Whether reading for information or for pleasure, you expect to
125 be able to comprehend what you are reading. You will be more motivated to read if what you read helps you in some way. Motivation can be increased by increasing your expected reward. Always
130 ask yourself what you hope to gain from each reading.

Most importantly, reading should be fun! You should look forward to reading and learning something new as you read. When
135 reading becomes a burden, you probably will not learn as you read. Your attitude will influence your motivation to read. Regularly check your attitude toward what you are reading and what you are learning. If reading
140 is not fun, try to find the reason and change it so you can enjoy reading.

Real Contexts is designed to help you accomplish your reading goals and move you toward greater proficiency in English.

ENDING TIME: _____ : _____
TOTAL TIME: _____
1000 WORDS ÷ _____ MIN = _____ WORDS/MIN

Write below three things you learned while reading *The Principles of ACTIVE Reading*. Share what you have learned with a partner.

_____

_____

_____

_____

_____

Calculate your approximate reading rate. Turn to Appendix B. Find your reading time in the left column. On the line coming down from the number 1 make a dot (•). Follow the time line across the page to the right column and the time is given in words-per-minute (wpm). The information from Appendices A, B, and C that were discussed in this passage will be used frequently as you read *Real Contexts*.

LANGUAGE LEARNING STRATEGIES

In this section, you will learn about the strategies you currently use. Complete the *Strategy Inventory for Language Learning*. Your language learning strategy profile will help you learn more about the kinds of strategies you use. This is not a test. There are no right or wrong answers to the questions. Give an answer that describes what you usually do. Your teacher will read through the directions with you.

Directions:

This form of the *Strategy Inventory for Language Learning (SILL)* is for students of English as a second or foreign language. You will find statements about learning English. Please read each statement. Write the response (l, 2, 3, 4 , or 5) that tells HOW TRUE OF YOU THE STATEMENT IS on the space before each item number.

1. Never or almost never true of me
2. Usually not true of me
3. Somewhat true of me
4. Usually true of me
5. Always or almost always true of me

NEVER OR ALMOST NEVER TRUE OF ME means that the statement is very rarely true of you.

USUALLY NOT TRUE OF ME means that the statement is true less than half the time.

SOMEWHAT TRUE OF ME means that the statement is true of you about half the time.

USUALLY TRUE OF ME means that the statement is true more than half the time.

ALWAYS OR ALMOST ALWAYS TRUE OF ME means that the statement is true of you almost always.

Answer in terms of how well the statement describes YOU. Do not answer how you think you should be, or what other people do. There are no right or wrong answers to these statements. Put your answers on a separate worksheet. Please make no marks on the items. Work as quickly as you can without being careless. This usually takes about 20–30 minutes to complete. If you have any questions, let the teacher know immediately.

EXAMPLE

_____ I actively seek out opportunities to talk with native speakers in English.

You have just completed the example item. Answer the rest of the items on the Worksheet on page 11.

STRATEGY INVENTORY FOR LANGUAGE LEARNING

1. Never or almost never true of me
2. Usually not true of me
3. Somewhat true of me
4. Usually true of me
5. Always or almost always true of me

Part A

_____ 1. I think of relationships between what I already know and new things I learn in English.

_____ 2. I use new English words in a sentence so I can remember them.

_____ 3. I connect the sound of a new English word and an image or picture of the word to help remember the word.

_____ 4. I remember a new English word by making a mental picture of a situation in which the word might be used.

_____ 5. I use rhymes to remember new English words.

_____ 6. I use flashcards to remember new English words.

_____ 7. I physically act out new English words.

_____ 8. I review English lessons often.

_____ 9. I remember new English words or phrases by remembering their location on the page, on the board, or on a street sign.

Part B

_____ 10. I say or write new English words several times.

_____ 11. I try to talk like native English speakers.

_____ 12. I practice the sounds of English.

_____ 13. I use the English words I know in different ways.

_____ 14. I start conversations in English.

_____ 15. I watch English language TV shows spoken in English or go to movies spoken in English.

_____ 16. I read for pleasure in English.

_____ 17. I write notes, messages, letters, or reports in English.

_____ 18. I first skim an English passage (read over the passage quickly) then go back and read carefully.

_____ 19. I look for words in my own language that are similar to new words in English.

_____ 20. I try to find patterns in English.

_____ 21. I find the meaning of an English word by dividing it into parts that I understand.

_____ 22. I try not to translate word-for-word.

_____ 23. I make summaries of information that I hear or read in English.

Part C

_____ 24. To understand unfamiliar English words, I make guesses.

_____ 25. When I can't think of a word during a conversation in English, I use gestures.

_____ 26. I make up new words if I do not know the right ones in English.

_____ 27. I read English without looking up every new word.

_____ 28. I try to guess what the other person will say next in English.

_____ 29. If I can't think of an English word, I use a word or phrase that means the same thing.

1. Never or almost never true of me
2. Usually not true of me
3. Somewhat true of me
4. Usually true of me
5. Always or almost always true of me

Part D

_____ 30. I try to find as many ways as I can to use my English.

_____ 31. I notice my English mistakes and use that information to help me do better.

_____ 32. I pay attention when someone is speaking English.

_____ 33. I try to find out how to be a better learner of English.

_____ 34. I plan my schedule so I will have enough time to study English.

_____ 35. I look for people I can talk to in English.

_____ 36. I look for opportunities to read as much as possible in English.

_____ 37. I have clear goals for improving my English skills.

_____ 38. I think about my progress in learning English.

Part E

_____ 39. I try to relax whenever I feel afraid of using English.

_____ 40. I encourage myself to speak English even when I am afraid of making a mistake.

_____ 41. I give myself a reward or treat when I do well in English.

_____ 42. I notice if I am tense or nervous when I am studying or using English.

_____ 43. I write down my feelings in a language learning diary.

_____ 44. I talk to someone else about how I feel when I am learning English.

Part F

_____ 45. If I do not understand something in English, I ask the other person to slow down or say it again.

_____ 46. I ask English speakers to correct me when I talk.

_____ 47. I practice English with other students.

_____ 48. I ask for help from English speakers.

_____ 49. I ask questions in English.

_____ 50. I try to learn about the culture of English speakers.

Version 7.0 (ESL/EFL) © R. Oxford, 1989

PROFILE OF RESULTS ON THE STRATEGY INVENTORY FOR LANGUAGE LEARNING (SILL)

You will receive a profile after you have finished the following work. This profile will show your SILL results. These results will tell you the kinds of strategies you use in learning English. There are no right or wrong answers.

To complete this profile, complete the following:

1. Copy your answers to the section below.
2. Add up each column. Put the result on the line marked SUM.
3. Divide by the number under SUM to get the average for each column. Round this average off to the nearest tenth, as in 3.4.
4. Figure out your overall average. To do this, add up all the SUMS for the different parts of the SILL. Then divide by 50.
5. When you have finished, transfer your averages to the graph and interpret your profile.

Part A	Part B	Part C	Part D	Part E	Part F	Whole SILL
1. ____	10. ____	24. ____	30. ____	39. ____	45. ____	SUM Part A ____
2. ____	11. ____	25. ____	31. ____	40. ____	46. ____	SUM Part B ____
3. ____	12. ____	26. ____	32. ____	41. ____	47. ____	SUM Part C ____
4. ____	13. ____	27. ____	33. ____	42. ____	48. ____	SUM Part D ____
5. ____	14. ____	28. ____	34. ____	43. ____	49. ____	SUM Part E ____
6. ____	15. ____	29. ____	35. ____	44. ____	50. ____	SUM Part F ____
7. ____	16. ____		36. ____			
8. ____	17. ____		37. ____			
9. ____	18. ____		38. ____			
	19. ____					
	20. ____					
	21. ____					
	22. ____					
	23. ____					

SUM ____	SUM ____	SUM ____	SUM ____	SUM ____	SUM ____	SUM ____
÷ 9 = ____	÷ 14 = ____	÷ 6 = ____	÷ 9 = ____	÷ 6 = ____	÷ 6 = ____	÷ 50 = ____

OVERALL AVERAGE

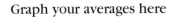

Graph your averages here

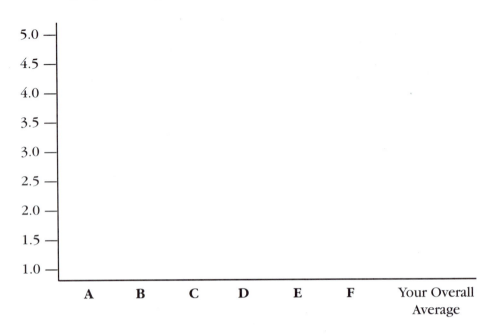

KEY TO UNDERSTANDING YOUR AVERAGES

HIGH	Always or almost always used	4.5 to 5.0
	Usually used	3.5 to 4.4
MEDIUM	Sometimes used	2.5 to 3.4
	Usually not used	1.5 to 2.4
LOW	Never or almost never used	1.0 to 1.4

Each of these six strategy categories will be used throughout *Real Contexts*. You will learn several strategies from each category that you can use to increase your use of language learning strategies.

Version 7.0 (ESL/EFL) © R. Oxford, 1989

LANGUAGE LEARNING STYLE

One final questionnaire to complete before continuing with *Real Contexts* is the Style Analysis Survey. This will give you information for a language learning style profile that will help you learn more about how you learn best. First, complete the Style Analysis Survey. This is not a test. There are no right or wrong answers to the questions. Give an answer that describes what you usually do. Your teacher will read through the directions with you.

STYLE ANALYSIS SURVEY FOR LANGUAGE LEARNING

SAS WORKSHEET

PURPOSE: The SAS is designed to assess your general approach to learning and working. It does not predict your behavior in every instance, but it is a clear indication of your overall preferences.

INSTRUCTIONS: For each item, write the number that represents your approach to learning. Complete all items. There are five major activities representing five different aspects of your learning and working style. At the end you will find a self-scoring key and an interpretation of the results.

TIMING: It generally takes 30 minutes to complete the SAS. Do not spend too much time on any item. Indicate your immediate response and move to the next item.

For each item, write your immediate response:

0 = Never, 1 = Sometimes, 2 = Very Often, 3 = Always

ACTIVITY 1: HOW I USE MY PHYSICAL SENSES TO STUDY OR WORK

_____ 1. I remember something better if I write it down.

_____ 2. I take lots of notes.

_____ 3. I can visualize pictures, numbers, words in my head.

_____ 4. I prefer to learn with video or TV more than with other media.

_____ 5. I underline or highlight the important parts I read.

_____ 6. I use color-coding to help me as I learn or work.

_____ 7. I need written directions for tasks.

_____ 8. I get distracted by background noises.

_____ 9. I have to look at people to understand what they say.

_____ 10. I am more comfortable when the walls where I study or work have posters and pictures.

_____ 11. I remember things better if I discuss them out loud.

_____ 12. I prefer to learn by listening to a lecture or a tape, rather than by reading.

_____ 13. I need oral directions for tasks.

_____ 14. Background sounds help me think.

_____ 15. I like to listen to music when I study or work.

_____ 16. I can easily understand what people say even if I can't see them.

_____ 17. I remember better what people say than what they look like.

_____ 18. I easily remember jokes I hear.

_____ 19. I can identify people by their voices.

_____ 20. When I turn on the TV, I listen to the sound rather than watching the screen.

_____ 21. I'd rather just start doing things rather than pay attention to directions.

_____ 22. I need frequent breaks when I work or study.

_____ 23. I move my lips when I read silently.

_____ 24. I avoid sitting at a desk when I don't have to.

_____ 25. I get nervous when I sit still too long.

_____ 26. I think better when I can move around.

_____ 27. Manipulating objects helps me to remember.

_____ 28. I enjoy building or making things.

_____ 29. I like a lot of physical activities.

_____ 30. I enjoy collecting cards, stamps, coins, or other things.

ACTIVITY 2: HOW I DEAL WITH OTHER PEOPLE

_____ 1. I prefer to work or study with others.

_____ 2. I make new friends easily.

_____ 3. I like to be in groups of people.

_____ 4. It is easy for me to talk to strangers.

_____ 5. I keep up with personal news about other people.

_____ 6. I like to stay late at parties.

_____ 7. Interactions with new people give me energy.

_____ 8. I remember people's names easily.

_____ 9. I have many friends and acquaintances.

_____ 10. Wherever I go, I develop contacts.

_____ 11. I prefer to work or study alone.

_____ 12. I am rather shy.

_____ 13. I prefer individual hobbies and sports.

_____ 14. It is hard for most people to get to know me.

_____ 15. People view me as more detached than sociable.

_____ 16. In a large group, I tend to keep silent.

_____ 17. Gatherings with lots of people tend to stress me.

_____ 18. I get nervous when dealing with new people.

_____ 19. I avoid parties if I can.

_____ 20. Remembering names is difficult for me.

ACTIVITY 3: HOW I HANDLE POSSIBILITIES

_____ 1. I have a vivid imagination.

_____ 2. I like to think of lots of new ideas.

_____ 3. I can think of many different solutions to a problem.

_____ 4. I like multiple possibilities and options.

_____ 5. I enjoy considering future events.

_____ 6. Following a step-by-step procedure bores me.

_____ 7. I like to discover things rather than have everything explained.

_____ 8. I consider myself original.

_____ 9. I am an ingenious person.

_____ 10. It feels fine if the teacher or boss changes the plan.

_____ 11. I am proud of being practical.

_____ 12. I behave in a down-to-earth way.

_____ 13. I am attracted to sensible people.

_____ 14. I prefer realism instead of new, untested ideas.

_____ 15. I prefer things presented in a step-by-step way.

_____ 16. I want a class or work session to follow a clear plan.

_____ 17. I like concrete facts, not speculation.

_____ 18. Finding hidden meanings is frustrating or irrelevant to me.

_____ 19. I prefer to avoid too many options.

_____ 20. I feel it is useless for me to think about the future.

ACTIVITY 4: HOW I APPROACH TASKS

_____ 1. I reach decisions quickly.

_____ 2. I am an organized person.

_____ 3. I make lists of things that I need to do.

_____ 4. I consult my list in order to get things done.

_____ 5. Messy, unorganized environments make me nervous.

_____ 6. I start tasks on time or early.

_____ 7. I get to places on time.

_____ 8. Deadlines help me organize work.

_____ 9. I enjoy a sense of structure.

_____ 10. I follow through with what I have planned.

_____ 11. I am a spontaneous person.

_____ 12. I like to just let things happen, not plan them.

_____ 13. I feel uncomfortable with a lot of structure.

_____ 14. I put off decisions as long as I can.

_____ 15. I have a messy desk or room.

_____ 16. I believe deadlines are artificial or useless.

_____ 17. I keep an open mind about things.

_____ 18. I believe that enjoying myself is the most important thing.

_____ 19. Lists of tasks make me feel tired or upset.

_____ 20. I feel fine about changing my mind.

ACTIVITY 5: HOW I DEAL WITH IDEAS

_____ 1. I prefer simple answers rather than a lot of explanations.

_____ 2. Too many details tend to confuse me.

_____ 3. I ignore details that do not seem relevant.

_____ 4. It is easy for me to see the overall plan or big picture.

_____ 5. I can summarize information rather easily.

_____ 6. It is easy for me to paraphrase what other people say.

_____ 7. I see the main point very quickly.

_____ 8. I am satisfied with knowing the major ideas without the details.

_____ 9. I can pull together (synthesize) things easily.

_____ 10. When I make an outline, I write down only the key points.

_____ 11. I prefer detailed answers instead of short answers.

_____ 12. It is difficult for me to summarize detailed information.

_____ 13. I focus on specific facts or information.

_____ 14. I enjoy breaking general ideas down into smaller pieces.

_____ 15. I prefer looking for differences rather than similarities.

_____ 16. I use logical analysis to solve problems.

_____ 17. My written outlines contain many details.

_____ 18. I become nervous when only the main ideas are presented.

_____ 19. I focus on the details rather than the big picture.

_____ 20. When I tell a story or explain something, it takes a long time.

What These Averages Mean for You

Transfer your answers to the spaces below and sum each column. Then read the interpretation of your language learning styles.

ACTIVITY 1: HOW I USE MY PHYSICAL SENSES TO STUDY OR WORK

1. _____	11. _____	21. _____
2. _____	12. _____	22. _____
3. _____	13. _____	23. _____
4. _____	14. _____	24. _____
5. _____	15. _____	25. _____
6. _____	16. _____	26. _____
7. _____	17. _____	27. _____
8. _____	18. _____	28. _____
9. _____	19. _____	29. _____
10. _____	20. _____	30. _____
SUM _____	SUM _____	SUM _____

> **Threads**
>
> **Do you learn best by listening, by reading or by active participation?**

The sum for items 1–10 is the score for your **visual style preference.**

The sum for items 11–20 is the score for your **auditory style preference.**

The sum for items 21–30 is the score for your **hands-on style preference.**

Based on these scores, rank order the numbers with the highest number listed first:

_____ highest score

_____

_____ lowest score

Your sensory preferences are likely to affect the way you learn a language best. For instance, if you are a visual person, you might rely on the sense of sight and feel more comfortable with reading than with oral activities. If you are an auditory learner, you might prefer listening or speaking activities to reading assignments. If you are a hands-on learner, you might benefit from doing projects and moving around the room a lot. If two or all three of your sensory preferences are equally strong, you are flexible enough to enjoy a wide variety of activities.

Your teacher can help you optimize your language learning by giving you activities that relate to your sensory preferences. On the other hand, activities that might not be quite as suited to your sensory preferences—for example, reading and writing exercises for an auditory person—will help you stretch beyond your ordinary *comfort zone*. Welcome activities that fit you to a *T*, but also welcome those that give you a chance to practice your less favored senses.

ACTIVITY 2: HOW I DEAL WITH OTHER PEOPLE

1. _____	11. _____
2. _____	12. _____
3. _____	13. _____
4. _____	14. _____
5. _____	15. _____
6. _____	16. _____
7. _____	17. _____
8. _____	18. _____
9. _____	19. _____
10. _____	20. _____
SUM _____	SUM _____

The sum for items 1–10 is your score for extroversion, the degree to which you get your energy from people and events outside of yourself.

The sum for items 11–20 is your score for introversion, which indicates the extent to which you receive your energy from ideas, feelings, or concepts inside yourself.

If one score is higher than the other, write that category here:

_____

(If both numbers are equal, write equal.)

If you scored high on extroversion, you might enjoy a wide range of social, interactive events in the language classroom—games, storytelling, role-plays, skits. If you are more introverted, you might like to do more independent work or enjoy working in pairs with someone you know well. If the numbers are equal, either type of activity suits you well.

ACTIVITY 3: HOW I HANDLE POSSIBILITIES

1. _____	11. _____
2. _____	12. _____
3. _____	13. _____
4. _____	14. _____
5. _____	15. _____
6. _____	16. _____
7. _____	17. _____
8. _____	18. _____
9. _____	19. _____
10. _____	20. _____
SUM _____	SUM _____

The sum for items 1–10 tells how intuitive you are in your learning.
The sum for items 11–20 shows how concrete/sequential you are.

If one score is higher than the other, write that category here:

_____

(If both numbers are equal, write equal.)

If you are intuitive, you might seek out the major principles or rules of language, like to speculate about possibilities (cultural or language-related), enjoy abstract thinking, and avoid step-by-step instruction. You are much more random in your approach than your concrete/sequential classmates, who are likely to prefer step-by-step language activities and who might engage in a variety of multimedia memory strategies. Equal scores for the two areas indicates an integration of the two modes.

ACTIVITY 4: HOW I APPROACH TASKS

1. ____   11. ____

2. ____   12. ____

3. ____   13. ____

4. ____   14. ____

5. ____   15. ____

6. ____   16. ____

7. ____   17. ____

8. ____   18. ____

9. ____   19. ____

10. ____   20. ____

SUM ____   SUM ____

The sum for items 1–10 shows how much you need closure, that is, how immediately you need to reach decisions and finish tasks.

The sum for items 11–20 reveals how much you need openness, that is, how much you need to delay reaching decisions and finishing tasks.

If one score is higher than the other, write that category here:

_____

(If both numbers are equal, write equal.)

If your score is higher for closure, you focus carefully on all tasks, meet deadlines, plan ahead for assignments, want explicit instruction, and ask for clear directions. If your score is higher for openness, you probably enjoy *discovery learning* in which you pick up information on your own, and you might prefer to relax and play with the language, without much concern for deadlines or planning ahead. Join forces with others who are not just like you, so you can learn to get things done while still having fun. If your results are equal for each part, you have already reached a good balance.

ACTIVITY 5: HOW I DEAL WITH IDEAS

1. ____	11. ____
2. ____	12. ____
3. ____	13. ____
4. ____	14. ____
5. ____	15. ____
6. ____	16. ____
7. ____	17. ____
8. ____	18. ____
9. ____	19. ____
10. ____	20. ____
SUM ____	SUM ____

The sum for items 1–10 gives your global score.
The sum for items 11–20 gives your analytic score.

If one score is higher than the other, write that category here:

_____

(If both numbers are equal, write equal.)

If you are more global, you might enjoy getting the main idea of a new-language conversation or a reading passage by guessing the meaning of unknown words and might like to use strategies (such as gestures or paraphrasing) for communicating even without knowing all the right phrases. But if you are more analytic, you might feel less comfortable with these rather holistic techniques and might focus more on language details, logical analysis of grammar points, and contrasts between English and your first language. Learn new techniques from those who are not as global or as analytic as you are. If your preferences are equal this shows harmony between global and analytic orientations.

A SNAPSHOT OF YOUR LANGUAGE LEARNING STYLE

Now that you have completed the interpretation for each section, summarize the major style characteristics that apply to you by circling the appropriate category. If for any single section some of your preferences are equal, circle all that are equal.

1. Your Sensory Preferences: Visual, Auditory, Hands-On

2. Your Relations With Others: Extroversion, Introversion

3. Your Relations With Ideas: Intuitive, Concrete/Sequential

4. Your Orientation To Learning Tasks: Closure, Openness

5. Your Overall Orientation: Global, Analytic

Each style preference offers significant strengths in learning a new language. No matter what your style preferences, you can capitalize on your strengths by recognizing and using them to your best advantage. You can also enhance your learning power by being aware of the style areas in which you feel less comfortable and by working on their development.

© R. Oxford, 1993

Are You Ready to Begin *Real Contexts?*

You have completed three questionnaires and read one passage in this first chapter. The information about your reading preferences, your initial reading rate, your language learning strategies, and your language learning style all provide important information that will help you and your teacher know how to improve your reading skills. Use this preliminary information to help you as you now read each of the passages in *Real Contexts*.

WHAT HAVE YOU LEARNED?

Think about the questionnaires you have completed. What have you learned about yourself? Write a few ideas below.

_____

_____

_____

_____

_____

_____

_____

Discuss with a partner what you have learned about yourself.

Sports: Are You Physically Active?

Write an answer to the following questions, then discuss your answers with others in your class. If you do not know anything about the topics to be discussed, it is okay to say that you do not know. Not knowing anything about a reading topic and recognizing that you do not, is okay.

LEARNING STRATEGY

Forming Concepts: Relying on what you already know improves your reading comprehension.

1. In this chapter you will read *Physical Activity and Public Health, On a Roll, Second Time Around,* and *Baseball's Enduring Hold On America.* What do you expect to learn about sports?

   _____
   _____
   _____
   _____
   _____

2. What sports do you participate in now? Are there any sports you would like to participate in but do not?

   _____
   _____
   _____
   _____

3. What is your current attitude about sports?

   _____
   _____
   _____
   _____
   _____

Threads

Monica Seles, the No. 1-ranked women's tennis player, was seriously injured when she was stabbed in the back by a spectator during a tournament in Hamburg, Germany, April 30, 1993. The attacker was apparently a fanatical fan of Seles' rival, Steffi Graf of Germany. Seles, who required lengthy rehabilitation and was unable to play for months, lost her No. 1 ranking to Graf June 3.

The World Almanac® and Book of Facts 1994

4. What do you already do to show that you are physically fit?

_____

_____

_____

_____

_____

_____

READING 1: PHYSICAL ACTIVITY AND PUBLIC HEALTH

Pre-Reading Discussion

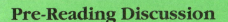

LEARNING STRATEGY

Managing Your Learning: Thinking about a topic before reading about it helps you to prepare for your reading assignments.

Discuss the following questions with members of your class.

1. Is it important that the *general public* be physically active? Why or why not?
2. Do you think there is a relationship between public health and physical activity?
3. Why do you think some people are not physically active?
4. What recommendation would you give as a general public guideline for physical activity?

LEARNING STRATEGY

Managing Your Learning: Reviewing vocabulary lets you prepare for new reading material.

Vocabulary Development: Crossword Making

Working with a partner and using the vocabulary below, take turns adding new words to the grid below, crossword fashion. Beginning with the word *marathon* in the middle of the grid, add additional words. Each word you add must connect with another word. All letters next to each other must form words. You will have three minutes to work together. You are not limited to the vocabulary below, add any additional vocabulary you know related to the topic of sports and outdoor activities.

Possible vocabulary:

lifestyle	race	baseball
health	athlete	football
exercise	walking	basketball
physical	running	flexibility
training	swimming	strength

Set a goal for the number of words-per-minute you want to achieve before reaching the end of this passage. Try to reach at least 200 words per minute. It might be helpful to review your reading rate from your weekly timed reading chart in Appendix B.

What is the reading rate goal for this reading?

Record that goal here: _____

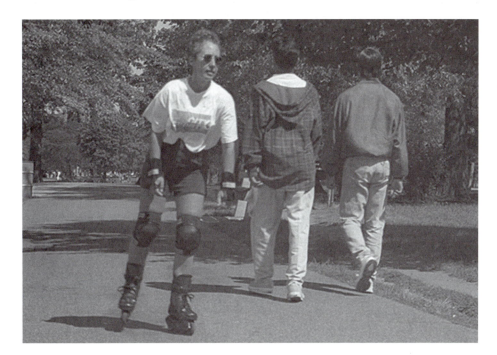

IT WORKS!
Learning Strategy:
Setting a Goal
for Improved
Reading Rate

Reading Skill Improvement

READING RATE INSTRUCTION

Rate Buildup Reading. You will be given 60 seconds to read as much material as you can from *Physical Activity and Public Health.* When your teacher says, *Stop,* write the number "1" above the word you are reading. You will begin reading again from the beginning of the text for an additional 60 seconds. Your goal is to read more material during the second 60-second period than in the first. When your teacher says, *Stop,* write the number "2" above the word you are reading. This reading rate improvement activity will be repeated a third and a fourth time. You are to write the numbers "3" and "4" above the word in the text that you reach after each 60-second period.

After the fourth minute, you will be allowed four additional minutes to complete reading the passage.

READING 1: PHYSICAL ACTIVITY AND PUBLIC HEALTH

by The American College of Sports and Medicine and the U.S. Centers for Disease Control and Prevention

Regular physical activity is an important component of a healthy lifestyle— preventing disease and enhancing health and quality of life. Evidence gathered over
5 the past several years, indicates that regular physical activity provides health benefits.

A primary benefit of regular physical activity is protection against coronary heart disease. In addition, physical activity appears
10 to provide some protection against several other chronic diseases such as adult-onset diabetes, hypertension, certain cancers, osteoporosis, and depression. Furthermore, on average, physically active people outlive
15 inactive people, even if they start their activity late in life. It is estimated that more than 250,000 deaths per year in the U.S. can be attributed to lack of regular physical activity, a number comparable to the deaths
20 attributed to other chronic disease risk factors such as obesity, high blood pressure, and elevated blood cholesterol.

Despite the recognized value of physical activity, few Americans are regularly active.
25 Only 22 percent of adults engage in leisure time physical activity at the level recommended for health benefits in *Healthy People 2000*. Fully 24 percent of adult Americans are completely inactive and are
30 badly in need of more physical activity. The remaining 54 percent are inadequately active and they too would benefit from more physical activity. Participation in regular physical activity appears to have greatly
35 increased during the 1960s, 1970s, and early 1980s, but has plateaued in recent years. Among ethnic minority populations, older persons, and those with lower incomes or levels of education, participation in regular
40 physical activity has remained consistently low.

Why are so few people physically active? Perhaps one answer is that previous public health efforts to promote physical activity
45 have overemphasized the importance of high-intensity exercise. The current low rate of participation may be explained, in part, by the perception of many people that they must engage in vigorous, continuous
50 exercise to reap health benefits. Actually the scientific evidence clearly demonstrates that regular, moderate-intensity physical activity provides substantial health benefits. A group of exercise and health experts provide the
55 following recommendation:

Every adult should accumulate 30 minutes or more of moderate-intensity physical activity over the course of most days of the week. Incorporating more
60 activity into the daily routine is an effective way to improve health. Activities that can contribute to the 30-minute total include walking up stairs (instead of taking the elevator),
65 gardening, raking leaves, dancing and walking part or all of the way to or from work. The recommended 30 minutes of physical activity may also come from planned exercise or recreation such as
70 jogging, playing tennis, swimming, and cycling. One specific way to meet the standard is to walk two miles briskly.

Because most adults fail to meet this recommended level of moderate-intensity
75 physical activity, almost all should strive to increase their participation in moderate or vigorous physical activity. Persons who currently do not engage in regular physical activity should begin by incorporating a few
80 minutes of increased activity into their day,

building up gradually to 30 minutes of additional physical activity. Those who are irregularly active should strive to adopt a more consistent pattern of activity.

85 Regular participation in physical activities that develop and maintain muscular strength and joint flexibility is also recommended.

This recommendation has been 90 developed to emphasize the important health benefits of moderate physical activity. But recognizing the benefits of physical activity is only part of the solution to this important public health problem. Today's 95 high-tech society entices people to be inactive. Cars, television, and labor-saving devices have profoundly changed the way many people perform their jobs, take care of their homes, and use their leisure time. 100 Furthermore, our surroundings often present significant barriers to participation in physical activity. Walking to the corner store proves difficult if there are no sidewalks; riding a bicycle to work is not an 105 option unless safe bike lanes or paths are available.

Many people will not change their lifestyles until the environmental and social barriers to physical activity are reduced or 110 eliminated. Individuals can help to overcome these barriers by modifying their own lifestyles and by encouraging family members and friends to become more active. In addition, public health agencies, 115 recreation boards, school groups, professional organizations, and fitness and sports organizations should work together to promote community, worksite, and school programs that help people become more 120 physically active.

Evaluate your reading rate performance.

1. How many lines of text did you read the first time? Write the number here: _____

2. Multiply the number of lines you read in the first one-minute segment by six. Write the product here: _____ (This is approximately the number of words that you read the first minute.)

IT WORKS!
Learning Strategy:
Evaluating Your
Reading Rate

3. How many lines of text did you read the fourth time? Write the number here: _____

4. Multiply the number of lines you read the fourth one-minute segment by six. Write the product here: _____ (This is approximately the number of words that you read the fourth minute.)

5. What was your reading rate goal? Write your goal here: _____

6. Compare the numbers in #2 and #4 with your goal in #5. How well did you do in accomplishing your reading rate goal?

Reading 1: Post-Reading Comprehension Check

LEARNING STRATEGY

Managing Your Learning: Discussing what you read helps you remember better.

1. With a different partner from the one you worked with in the pre-reading activity, discuss the same four questions.
2. What vocabulary did you encounter from the crossword-making activity?
3. Compare the advice given in this passage with your own attitude about physical fitness and your personal fitness plans.

Pre-Reading Discussion

This next reading passage is going to look at sports in perhaps a different way. *On A Roll* discusses two world-class athletes: Jean Driscoll and Jim Knaub.

The passage is divided into sections. You will be asked to make four predictions and you will be given a chance to confirm your predictions after reading a section of the text. Working with a partner can help you with the reading strategy of making predictions.

LEARNING STRATEGY

Forming Concepts: Predicting text content helps you as you read and confirming your predictions helps you make better predictions.

FIRST PREDICTION

Based on the title, *On A Roll,* what do you think this passage will be about?

READING 2: ON A ROLL

by Donna M. Tocci

"Train hard, rest hard, race hard." That is one motto Jim Knaub is living by this year.

Jean Driscoll spends so much time training for the next big race that she sacrifices most of her leisure time.

5   If these sound like the stories of any dedicated athlete you've ever read about, you're correct. Knaub and Driscoll are both world-class athletes:

PAUSE/SECOND PREDICTION

What sport do Knaub and Driscoll participate in?

Threads

Noureddine Morceli of Algeria broke the world record in the mile, Sept. 5, 1993 with a time of three minutes 44.39 seconds at a meet in Rieti, Italy. Morceli took nearly two seconds off the old record, set by Steve Cram in 1985.

The World Almanac® and Book of Facts 1994

Threads

**Sites of
Summer Olympic Games**

1896
Athens, Greece

1900
Paris, France

1904
St. Louis, MO

1906
Athens, Greece

1908
London, England

1912
Stockholm, Sweden

1920
Antwerp, Belgium

1924
Paris, France

1928
Amsterdam, Netherlands

1932
Los Angeles, CA

1936
Berlin, Germany

1948
London, England

1952
Helsinki, Finland

1956
Melbourne, Australia

1960
Rome, Italy

1964
Tokyo, Japan

1968
Mexico City, Mexico

1972
Munich, W. Germany

1976
Montreal, Canada

1980
Moscow, USSR

1984
Los Angeles, CA

1988
Seoul, S. Korea

1992
Barcelona, Spain

1996
Atlanta, GA

The World Almanac® and Book
of Facts 1994

They are Boston Marathon champions.

PAUSE/CONFIRM

Was your prediction correct? What clues helped you to predict?

10 Jean Driscoll has won Boston each of the four times she has competed. Jim Knaub has won a total of five times over an 11-year period. Both Knaub and Driscoll have set world records four times, including the 1993 winning times of 1:22:17 and 1:34:40, respectively.

Wheelchair racing has come a long way since the inaugural Boston
15 Marathon in 1975, when Bob Hall was the lone competitor along the 26.2 mile course. Most people who saw him pushing his heavy chair probably looked at him and thought how courageous and heartwarming this novelty was. Oh, how times have changed! Hall is still racing, but he is also coordinator of the most prestigious wheelchair race in the world.
20 The race that started with one competitor now attracts an international field of more than 80 athletes.

Wheelchair racing has undergone many changes, most noticeably in the public's attitude. Most people no longer see it as a nice little race for disabled people before the real runners come down the road. They now
25 see exactly what they should see—dedicated, competitive athletes. Each has his or her own training schedule and style, but make no mistake: every athlete is out to win and show the world that this sport is just that—a sport.

PAUSE/THIRD PREDICTION

What kind of special training do you think wheelchair athletes have to do to prepare for a marathon?

Jean Driscoll trains with her alma mater, the University of Illinois. The
30 school has a highly competitive racing team under the coaching of Marty Morse. For speed, Driscoll works out daily with the men's team. She finds it a "luxury" to train with the men even though they are far ahead of her some days.

"I can use them as goals," she says. "It's a benefit to have other people
35 to push you."

The team trains on the flatlands of southern Illinois. It is here that the athletes practice drafting (shielding oneself from the wind behind another athlete) and race strategy. Because it isn't hilly, the wind blows very hard. Fighting against the wind can simulate climbing a hill.
40 Driscoll believes her success is due to the support she gets from the team atmosphere and the dedication of Morse, her coach. He is involved in every aspect of her racing—from the size of her chair to the design of the gloves she uses when she is pushing. She think Morse's master's degree in exercise physiology is the key to his understanding athletes and their training.

PAUSE/CONFIRM

Is the wheelchair training you predicted used by Driscoll? What clues helped you?

PAUSE/FOURTH PREDICTION

Do you think that Driscoll uses the same training schedule?

45 Whereas Driscoll relies heavily on her coach and team support, Jim Knaub is his own coach. He trains with others on occasion, but his philosophy is totally different.
"I gain most benefit alone. I race best alone and by myself. Training alone, I am psychologically prepared to do that," say the Southern Californian. It is evident in the way he races—he moves quickly to the
50 front, and in most cases all alone, just the way he likes it.
Knaub's general training takes him to the streets six days a week. He lifts weights, usually three days a week. Knaub's training is very specific when it comes to preparing for Boston: he does less long, slow distance and more specialized training. "Obviously I do a lot of hills," says Knaub.
55 "I coast better than a lot of people, and I am climbing better than ever." He believes his climbing ability is one of the main reasons for his continued success at Boston. The race may be won or lost on the uphill climb. This is a focus in training for Knaub.

PAUSE/CONFIRM

Is the wheelchair training you predicted used by Knaub? What clues helped you to predict?

60 As public interest in wheelchair racing continues to grow, the people making it happen have to look to the future. No matter how long Knaub and Driscoll keep racing, they will continue to work for the betterment of the sport and the education of the public. Knaub sums up what they would both like people to know: "Don't put the wheelchair before the athlete."

PAUSE/CONFIRM

The first prediction you made was based on the title of the passage. Was your prediction correct? What clues helped you?

Threads

Sites of
Winter Olympic Games:

1924
Chamonix, France

1928
St. Moritz, Switzerland

1932
Lake Placid, N.Y.

1936
Garmisch-Partenkirchen,
Germany

1948
St. Moritz, Switzerland

1952
Oslo, Norway

1956
Cortina d'Ampezzo, Italy

1960
Squaw Valley, CA.

1964
Innsbruck, Austria

1968
Grenoble, France

1972
Sapporo, Japan

1976
Innsbruck, Austria

1980
Lake Placid, N.Y.

1984
Sarajevo, Yugoslavia

1988
Calgary, Alberta

1992
Albertville, France

1994
Lillehammer, Norway

2002
Salt Lake City, UT

The World Almanac® and Book
of Facts 1994

LEARNING STRATEGY

Managing Your Learning: Scanning is a reading skill to help you locate specific information.

Reading 2: Post-Reading Comprehension Check

Scan the passage, *On A Roll,* for the following information. After finding the information, check your answers with a partner.

1. In 1993, what was Driscoll's winning time?

_____

2. In 1993, what was Knaub's winning time?

_____

3. When was the first wheelchair marathon race?

_____

4. Who was the first wheelchair racer in the Boston Marathon?

_____

5. How many international athletes now participate in the Boston Marathon Wheelchair race?

_____

6. What is one change that has occurred in wheelchair racing?

_____

7. Where does Jean Driscoll do her training?

_____

8. Why does Driscoll like to train with the men's team at the University of Illinois?

_____

9. Who does Driscoll rely on to help her with her training?

_____

10. Who does Knaub rely on to help him with his training?

_____

LEARNING STRATEGY

Personalizing: Identifying yourself with a person in a story helps you to understand the material better because it becomes more real to you.

1. Did you know much about wheelchair racing before reading this text?
2. What is one thing you would ask Jean Driscoll or Jim Knaub if you were to interview them?
3. Do you know a handicapped person who is athletic? Does his or her handicap limit his or her participation in sports?

Pre-Reading Discussion

LEARNING STRATEGY

Remembering New Material: Thinking of what you have already read makes you remember new material better and longer.

You will now read a second passage about Jim Knaub, the wheelchair racer. Think about what you already know about Jim Knaub. Share one idea with a partner in your class. What other sports can people in wheelchairs participate in?

Reading Skill Improvement

READING RATE INSTRUCTION

Class paced reading. We are going to read this passage at a minimal reading rate of 150 words-per-minute. As you read, the teacher will call out the numbers one through 3.25. Each time the teacher calls out a number you should be near the same bold-faced number in the margin. If you are not at the bold-faced number when the teacher calls it, skip from where you are currently reading to the number. Do everything you can to keep up with the minimal reading rate of 150 words-per-minute.

If you pass a bold faced number before the teacher calls it, keep reading. You are reading faster than 150 words-per-minute. Keep up with the minimal reading rate goal.

READING 3: SECOND TIME AROUND

by Bob Babbitt

It's amazing how quickly life can change. One minute you're 22 years old, one of America's top pole vaulters, a limitless future ahead of you. The next? Three thousand
5 pounds of metal is heading in your direction and there is nothing you can do about it.

Jim Knaub definitely had Olympic potential. He had the ability to be a great vaulter, and the physical attributes to be a
10 world record holder. But his crushed spine from a motorcycle accident changed all that.

David Bailey was one of the top motocross racers in the world. He was making $700,000 a year, had a big contract
15 with the motorcycle company Honda, owned a ranch in Virginia, a home in Los Angeles and received hundreds of pieces of fan mail a week. Bailey was considered the smoothest rider on the circuit, a guy who
20 was never out of control. When he was 25 **1** years old, David Bailey tried a dangerous jump. Like Knaub, he ended up in a wheelchair.

During the time since their accidents,
25 both Knaub and Bailey have become wheelchair racers, two of the best. Knaub, the veteran, is the more accomplished of the two, having won the Boston Marathon five times and the Los Angeles Marathon twice.
30 Bailey is a rookie; he entered the world of wheelchair racing in the spring of 1991. He won the DisneyWorld Marathon last winter and had the racing world speculating about the new kid on the block.
35 After his injury, Bailey was in total denial. He would say that tomorrow he would get up and everything would be okay.

He felt he wouldn't be in a wheelchair for long. If everyone would just leave him alone,
40 he'd be just fine. David Bailey had never met an obstacle that he couldn't overcome.

Knaub learned about David Bailey and **2** offered to help. David thanked him for calling, and told Knaub he didn't
45 understand. "I'll be walking in about a week and a half. I have all these machines . . . I'm going to get better," David said.

"You don't understand" has become the joke between them. From their first
50 meeting, Bailey was constantly saying, "But you don't understand" every time Knaub told him to get on with his life, to enjoy what he has.

David Bailey spent three years feeling
55 sorry for himself. Jim Knaub offered him a new life—the opportunity to be physical again, to use a wheelchair, to be independent.

Knaub considers his real victories the
60 people he is able to help, not the marathon races he wins.

Once he made the commitment to racing a chair, Bailey reverted to his old self, analyzing video, lifting weights, and
65 setting short and longterm goals. At first, he called Knaub constantly, asking for **3** advice.

Bailey has come a long way. He now thinks he might be able to help other people
70 going through what he went through. He says, "If I can go out and race, have a good time, and influence people's lives the way that Jim has influenced mine, that would be great." **3.25**

Managing Your Learning: Self-evaluating your reading helps you work toward your goal of increasing your rate.

Use these questions to evaluate your reading rate progress:

1. Were you able to keep your reading rate at 150 wpm?

YES   NO

2. Did you go faster than 150 wpm?

YES   NO

3. Is maintaining a rate of 150 wpm getting easier for you?

YES   NO

Why? _____

4. Is maintaining a rate of 150 wpm still difficult?

YES   NO

Why? _____

Reading 3: Post-Reading Comprehension Check

Remembering New Material: Discussing what you read helps you remember better.

Discuss the following questions with a partner.

1. What kind of a person is Jim Knaub? What clues in the text help you to know this?

2. Do you know someone like Knaub, who helps other people in difficult situations?

3. What is the significance of the title, Second Time Around?

READING 4: BASEBALL'S ENDURING HOLD ON AMERICA

LEARNING STRATEGY

Learning with Others: Talking with others prior to reading helps you prepare to understand.

Baseball is perhaps one of the most well-known sports in the world. Discuss the following questions as a class:

1. What do you know about the game of baseball?
2. Where did baseball begin as a sport?
3. Which baseball players do you know about?
4. Which baseball teams do you know about?
5. Have you ever played baseball?
6. Do you like baseball? Why? Why not?
7. Do most Americans you are acquainted with know how to play baseball?

IT WORKS!
Learning Strategy:
Setting a Reading
Rate Goal

GOAL SETTING

Set a goal for the number of words-per-minute you want to reach while reading *Baseball's Enduring Hold on America.* Record that goal here: _____

What is the reading comprehension goal for this reading?

Record that goal here: _____

READING 4: BASEBALL'S ENDURING HOLD ON AMERICA

by Jim Ballard

Because of its ability to create lasting memories, baseball holds a special place in the hearts of many people. "I think baseball's attraction, in part, is the fact that it
5 establishes a kind of clarity in the game between the players," indicates Benjamin Rader, a University of Nebraska-Lincoln history professor and author of *Baseball: A History of America's Game.* They are
10 separated from each other on a large green field, so it's much easier to remember what happened in a baseball game; it forms memories very clearly.

"That clarity also comes from the slow
15 pace of the game, allowing time to analyze what's happened, as compared to the action in basketball, which is so fast that it is difficult to remember a sequence of events. So baseball is ideally suited for history, for
20 memories of the past."

Jules Tygiel, a San Francisco State University history professor and author of *Baseball's Great Experiment: Jackie Robinson and His Legacy,* writes about the
25 game's historical significance: "I would say certainly from the 1860s through the TV age, even into the 1950s and 1960s, baseball was truly the number one American pastime. It really was the athletic event that
30 captured the imaginations, dominated the sport pages, and people really lived and died with." He maintains that the other major sports—basketball and football in particular—needed the power of television
35 to gain the type of following and cultural impact baseball enjoyed. Because it coincided with the Industrial Revolution and with improvements in transportation and communication, baseball was allowed to be
40 publicized and its influence to be expanded into playing an unusual role in American society during almost a 100-year period.

Larry Gerlach, who teaches a history of baseball class at Utah State University and is
45 author of *The Man in Blue: A Conversation with Baseball Umpires* concurs, "Baseball has held a special fascination because it is the oldest recognized sport. It was both a reflection on American society and a social
50 cultural agent impacting American society. There is hardly a thing in American history after the Civil War that is not present in sport generally, and baseball in particular. We began to deal with the issues of racism,
55 sexism, ethnicity, and economic organization in the industry of baseball."

Rader points out, though, that baseball has a questionable origin. Despite the argument that it was founded by Abner
60 Doubleday, it is more likely an adaptation of boys' games played in England at the time of colonization. "Professional baseball itself propagated a myth that baseball was created in Cooperstown in 1839. This was done
65 mainly to popularize the sport, but also to separate it from England, and to clearly establish it as 'America's game.'"

Baseball may not have its beginning in the U. S., but its past is one that interests and
70 fascinates historians because of the statistics and folklore that surround the game. Even before educators discovered the sport as a legitimate field of history, there was a legitimate story of baseball. Rader, Tygiel,
75 Gerlach, and many of their colleagues are getting into that history to evaluate and understand more about America's pastime.

Fans love to debate questions such as the cause of the deadball era or which team
80 was the greatest of all time. Yet, one thing remains constant, and that is the game itself.

"Baseball has not changed," maintains Tygiel. "We can point to the individual rule changes, the designated hitter, even to

85 things like changing the pattern of the stadiums which have played a major role in the way the game is played more recently, but it's essentially the same game. It's still nine people out in the field, it's still the

90 pitcher versus the hitter, and that's part of the enduring charm of it."

Gerlach agrees. "Baseball has not changed to the degree that other sports have. The rules from the 1890s to present

95 are virtually identical, whereas football, basketball, and most other sports are continually undergoing a change in the rules and the nature of the game. And the statistical continuity has provided a structure

100 whereby scholars, in a meaningful sense, can interpret and compare different eras of different players. You don't find football and basketball people that are conscious of statistics, either individual or career, that you

105 find with baseball people."

Rader points out that players were better known and more respected in the past. Lou Gehrig, Rogers Hornsby, and Joe DiMaggio had huge followings and were, in

110 their eras, among the most well-known people in the world. Modern-day stars aren't highly regarded.

Tygiel feels television is a major reason why players are not as respected as they

115 once were. It subjects athletes to greater pressure, so they're not allowed to be just "ball-players" and therefore can't be seen as role models to be emulated and adored. "We see today's players more in many ways. We

120 see them on TV so everybody knows their faces; we see them regularly in close-up profiles that people 50 years ago never did. Reporting is also different. They probe into the players' personal lives, and record

125 everything they do. If Babe Ruth were alive today, the newspapers wouldn't be big enough to sustain all of his exploits."

However, Rader sees today's ballplayers possessing far superior athletic skills than

130 their predecessors. "My belief is that athletes today simply have to be better. And they are better despite the crying you hear from sportswriters and others."

Baseball always has and likely will

135 continue to be considered America's favorite pastime. Though the game has changed little over the decades, it has created a history unique from other sports. Each year, as the grayness of winter turns to the promises of

140 spring, baseball is leading the charge. "It's ideally suited for history, for memories of the past," Rader asserts. "And I think it's uniquely a summer game, in a sense that we identify baseball with a coming of a new

145 season, the coming of spring and warm weather, a new beginning."

Reading 4: Post-Reading Comprehension Check

Without looking back at the passage *Baseballs' Enduring Hold on America,* answer the following comprehension questions.

1. Why is baseball such a popular sport in America?
   a. It is a sport that started in the United States.
   b. Baseball fans have good memories of baseball games.
   c. Baseball historians have kept a record of the sport.
   d. It was the first sport to be on TV.

2. It is easier to remember the events of a baseball game because
   a. of the slow pace of the game.
   b. the TV can show the instant replays.
   c. historians record the game.
   d. the statistics are easily available.

3. Unlike football and basketball, baseball did not
   a. develop until the Industrial Revolution.
   b. have an influence on the culture of society.
   c. catch the attention of the public in its early history.
   d. need TV to make it popular with the public.

4. Baseball is considered
   a. the sport of the Civil War.
   b. the oldest known sport.
   c. to be a good sport for TV.
   d. to be the most important sport.

5. Some people say that baseball first began
   a. as a sport to separate America from England.
   b. as America's game when TV was invented.
   c. as a game in England played by young boys.
   d. as a pastime during the Civil War.

6. The story of baseball is so interesting that
   a. historians are doing more research about the game.
   b. players are easily recognized on TV.
   c. the changes of the game have been publicized.
   d. books are written to record the statistics.

7. One difference between baseball and other sports is that

  a. fans love the game more than any other sport.

  b. the rules of the games have changed significantly over the years.

  c. the players are more recognized than players in other sports.

  d. baseball is basically the same game today that it was several years ago.

8. Baseball statistics allow us to

  a. easily write the history of the game.

  b. keep track of how the game has changed over time.

  c. compare different teams and different players.

  d. compare it with other sports.

9. Compared with players from several years ago, players today are

  a. more famous.

  b. seen on TV.

  c. younger and taller.

  d. better athletes.

10. Baseball is often associated with

  a. the start of a new season.

  b. the history of other great sports.

  c. passing the time quietly.

  d. famous players from TV.

Total number of correct answers: _____ / 10

Record your reading comprehension score on the comprehension chart in Appendix C.

READING STRATEGY CHECKLIST

Check off the strategies you used while reading and answering the questions.

_____ I used my general knowledge of the topic while reading and answering the questions.

_____ I skipped words I do not know.

_____ I used my knowledge of prefixes and suffixes to guess the meaning of words I did not know.

_____ I chose my answer by eliminating choices that did not seem reasonable.

_____ Others? Write them here: _____

_____

_____

IT WORKS!
Learning Strategy:
Self-Evaluating

Managing Your Learning: Evaluating your reading rate helps you improve it.

Record your reading rate on the graph in Appendix B. How does your reading rate on this passage compare with your rate on the other passages? Slower? Faster? The same?

Did you reach the reading rate goal you set before reading?

Each of the comprehension questions above can be classified into one of three reading comprehension categories:

- Understanding Main Ideas,
- Understanding Direct Statements, or
- Understanding Inferences.

Review your performance on each question and record your performance on the chart provided in Appendix C. How does your reading comprehension on this passage compare with the previous passages? Lower? Higher? The same?

Did you reach the reading comprehension goal you set before reading?

After checking your answers, review each one that you marked incorrectly and determine WHY you missed the question.

POST-READING EVALUATION

Managing Your Learning: Evaluate what you have learned in this chapter.

Respond in writing to the following questions, then discuss your answers with others in your class.

1. What have you learned from all the readings in this chapter on sports?

_____

_____

_____

_____

_____

2. How has your knowledge changed as a result of these readings?

_____

_____

_____

_____

_____

3. How has your attitude changed as a result of these readings?

_____

_____

_____

_____

_____

4. What can you do to show that you are more aware of sports or that you are more physically fit?

_____

_____

_____

_____

_____

Education: What Are Your Goals?

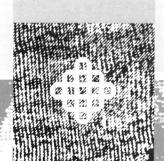

Complete the following statement by checking the goals you want to achieve in this chapter.

While working on this chapter, I will make an effort to:

_____ **1.** increase my reading rate.

_____ **2.** increase my comprehension of main ideas.

_____ **3.** increase my comprehension of direct statements.

_____ **4.** increase my comprehension of inferences.

_____ **5.** improve my vocabulary.

_____ **6.** learn more about the information in this chapter.

_____ **7.** be more aware of my reading strategies.

_____ **8.** ask more questions when I don't understand what I read.

READING 1: THE UNITED STATES OF AMERICA NATIONAL EDUCATION GOALS 2000

Pre-Reading Discussion

LEARNING STRATEGY

Forming Concepts: Reviewing vocabulary helps you increase your reading rate and comprehension.

Complete the following crossword puzzle using words that describe things at school. A vocabulary word bank has been provided for you.

Wordbank

blackboard	book	bookstore	classrooms	chairs
computer	crayons	desk	eraser	homework
library	notebook	paper	pencil	stapled
students	tape	teacher	telephone	

Across

2. Don't use a pen, use a _____.
4. I am reading a good _____.
5. I am almost out of _____. I need to go to the bookstore to buy more.
6. Used to hang pictures.
8. I write notes in this.
9. The teacher is writing on the _____.
11. Many books are in this building.
14. May I use the _____ to call my family?
15. He _____ the pages of the lesson together so that we wouldn't lose them.
16. She has a new box of _____. There are 48 colors in her box.
17. There are eight students and one _____ in the classroom.
18. There are 20 _____ and 22 students in the classroom.
19. How many _____ are there in your school?

Down

1. The student is seated at a _____.
3. I need a _____ to help me with my homework.
7. You use this to clean the blackboard.
10. The teacher gives us _____ every night.
12. I buy books here.
13. There are eight _____ and one teacher in the classroom.

© 1995 by Alta Book Center Publishers

Personalizing: Working with classmates provides a way to check your work.

Check your answers with a partner.

As a class, discuss the vocabulary from the crossword puzzle. Review each word and write as many synonyms as you can for each. Can you list additional vocabulary that is used at school? Share your list of additional vocabulary.

Threads

What sculpture is to a block of marble, education is to a human soul.

Joseph Addison (1672–1719), English essayist

School Vocabulary	Synonyms
blackboard	_____
book	_____
bookstore	_____
classrooms	_____
chairs	_____
computer	_____
crayons	_____
desk	_____
eraser	_____
homework	_____
library	_____
notebook	_____
paper	_____
pencil	_____
stapled	_____
students	_____
tape	_____
teacher	_____
telephone	_____

Additional school vocabulary

_____

_____

_____

_____

_____

_____

**Managing Your Learning: Working with classmates helps
you develop your language skills.**

As a class, briefly discuss the following questions:

1. What is a standard?
2. Do you think it is important to have national educational standards?
   Why? Why not?
3. Does your country of origin have national education standards?
4. Do you think there should be international standards for education?
   Why? Why not?

Review your reading rate from your weekly timed reading chart in
Appendix B.

What is the reading rate goal for this passage?

Record that goal here: _____

IT WORKS!
Learning Strategy:
Setting a Reading
Rate Goal

Reading Skill Improvement

READING RATE INSTRUCTION

Rate Buildup Reading. You will be given 60 seconds to read as much
material as you can from *The United States of America National
Education Goals 2000.* When your teacher says, *Stop,* write the number
"1" above the word you are reading. You will begin reading again from the
beginning of the text for an additional 60 seconds. Your goal is to read
more material during the second 60-second period than in the first. When
your teacher says, *Stop,* write the number "2" above the word you are
reading. This reading rate improvement drill will be repeated a third and a
fourth time. You are to write the numbers "3" and "4" above the word in
the text that you reach after each 60-second period.

After the fourth minute, your instructor will allow you additional time
if needed to complete reading the passage.

READING 1: THE UNITED STATES OF AMERICA NATIONAL EDUCATION GOALS 2000

By the Year 2000—

- ALL CHILDREN in America will start school ready to learn.

5 • THE HIGH SCHOOL graduation rate will increase to at least 90 percent.

- ALL STUDENTS will leave grades 4, 8, and 12 having demonstrated competency over challenging subject matter including English, mathematics,
10 science, foreign languages, civics and government, economics, the arts, history, and geography, and every school in America will ensure that all students learn to use their minds well, so they
15 may be prepared for responsible citizenship, further learning, and productive employment in our nation's modern economy.

- UNITED STATES students will be first in
20 the world in mathematics and science achievement.

- EVERY ADULT American will be literate and will possess the knowledge and skills necessary to compete in a global
25 economy and exercise the rights and responsibilities of citizenship.

- EVERY SCHOOL in the United States will be free of drugs, violence, and the unauthorized presence of firearms and
30 alcohol and will offer a disciplined environment conducive to learning.

- THE NATION'S teaching force will have access to programs for the continued improvement of their professional skills
35 and the opportunity to acquire the knowledge and skills needed to instruct and prepare all American students for the next century.

- EVERY SCHOOL will promote
40 partnerships that will increase parental involvement and participation in promoting the social, emotional, and academic growth of children.

Evaluate your reading rate performance.

1. How many lines of text did you read the first time? Write the number here: _____

2. Multiply the number of lines you read in the first one-minute segment by 6. Write the product here: _____ (This is approximately the number of words that you read the first minute.)

3. How many lines of text did you read the fourth time? Write the number here: _____

4. Multiply the number of lines you read the fourth one-minute segment by 6. Write the product here: _____ (This is approximately the number of words that you read the fourth minute.)

5. What was your reading rate goal? Write your goal here: _____

6. Compare the numbers in #2 and #4 with your goal in #5. How well did you do in accomplishing your reading rate goal?

IT WORKS!
Learning Strategy:
Evaluating Your
Reading Rate

Reading 1: Post-Reading Comprehension Check

LEARNING STRATEGY

Understanding and Using Emotions: Discussing your attitude toward a topic can help to clarify your thoughts about what you read.

With a partner, discuss your personal reaction to the proposed U.S. national education standards you have just read about.

LEARNING STRATEGY

Forming Concepts: Writing about what you read helps you understand your reading.

Review each of the proposed U.S. national education goals for the year 2000. Why do you think these goals are important for the U.S. Education system? Write your ideas below.

_____

_____

_____

_____

_____

_____

_____

IT WORKS!
Learning Strategy:
Rely on What
You Know

Think about the U.S. National Education Goals for the year 2000. Are any of these goals important for the education system in your country? Write eight goals for national education for your country. (This activity could be done in groups by nationality.)

1. _____

   _____

2. _____

   _____

3. _____

   _____

4. _____

   _____

5. _____

   _____

6. _____

   _____

7. _____

   _____

8. _____

   _____

Pre-Reading Discussion

Managing Your Learning: Thinking about a topic before reading about it helps you to prepare for your reading assignment.

Think about the following questions prior to reading the fictional story, *Charles,* by Shirley Jackson.

1. Do you remember the first day you went to school? How old were you? What did you wear? How did you feel? Nervous? Excited?
2. Did you go to school with your friends (children you knew before starting school) or did you go not knowing who you would meet?
3. Did your parents know the parents of your classmates?

Managing Your Learning: Reviewing important vocabulary will help you during your reading.

Review the following vocabulary. Do you know these words? What part of speech is each word? A noun? A verb? Label each word and use each in a sentence. Before reading, also remember the school vocabulary reviewed at the beginning of this chapter.

kindergarten	institution	renounce	enormously
corduroy	to kick	era	insanely
overalls	to throw out	swagger	reformation
to be fresh	anxious	raucous	
to spank	P.T.A.	insolently	

READING 2: CHARLES

by Shirley Jackson

The day my son Laurie started kindergarten he renounced corduroy overalls with bibs and began wearing blue jeans with a belt; I watched him go off the first morning with the older girl next door, seeing clearly that an era of my life was ended, my sweet-voiced nursery-school tot
5   replaced by a long-trousered, swaggering character who forgot to stop at the corner and wave good-bye to me.

He came home the same way, the front door slamming open, his cap on the floor, and the voice suddenly become raucous shouting, "Isn't anybody *here?*"
10   At lunch he spoke insolently to his father, spilled his baby sister's milk, and remarked that his teacher said we were not to take the name of the Lord in vain.

"How *was* school today?" I asked, elaborately casual.

"All right," he said.
15   "Did you learn anything?" his father asked.

Laurie regarded his father coldly. "I didn't learn nothing," he said.

"Anything," I said. "Didn't learn anything."

"The teacher spanked a boy, though," Laurie said, while eating his bread and butter. "For being fresh," he added, with his mouth full.
20   "What did he do?" I asked. "Who was it?"

Laurie thought. "It was Charles," he said. "He was fresh. The teacher spanked him and made him stand in a corner. He was awfully fresh."

"What did he do?" I asked again, but Laurie slid off his chair, took a cookie, and left, while his father was still saying, "See here, young man."
25   The next day Laurie remarked at lunch, as soon as he sat down, "Well, Charles was bad again today." He grinned enormously and said, "Today Charles hit the teacher."

"Good heavens," I said, mindful of the Lord's name. "I suppose he got spanked again?"
30   "He sure did," Laurie said. "Look up," he said to his father.

"What?" his father said, looking up.

"Look down," Laurie said. "Look at my thumb. Gee, you're dumb." He began to laugh insanely.

"Why did Charles hit the teacher?" I asked quickly.
35   "Because she tried to make him color with red crayons," Laurie said. "Charles wanted to color with green crayons so he hit the teacher and she spanked him and said nobody play with Charles but everybody did."

The third day—it was Wednesday of the first week—Charles bounced a see-saw on to the head of a little girl and made her bleed, and the
40   teacher made him stay inside all during recess. Thursday Charles had to stand in a corner during story-time because he kept pounding his feet on the floor. Friday Charles was deprived of blackboard privileges because he threw chalk.

LEARNING STRATEGY

Personalizing: Identifying with a person in a story helps you to understand the material better because it becomes more real to you.

As a class, discuss the following questions:

1. What do you think of Laurie's behavior at home?
2. Do you think that his transition to kindergarten has been difficult?
3. What do you think about Laurie's classmate, Charles?
4. Did you ever experience a similar situation when you started school?

Continue reading the story:

On Saturday I remarked to my husband, "Do you think kindergarten is too unsettling for Laurie? All this toughness, and bad grammar, and this
45 Charles boy sounds like such a bad influence."

"It'll be all right," my husband said reassuringly. "Bound to be people like Charles in the world. Might as well meet them now as later."

On Monday Laurie came home late, full of news. "Charles," he shouted as he came up the hill; I was waiting anxiously on the front steps.
50 "Charles," Laurie yelled all the way up the hill, "Charles was bad again."

"Come right in," I said, as soon as he came close enough. "Lunch is waiting."

"You know what Charles did?" he demanded, following me through the door. "Charles yelled so in school they sent a boy in from first grade
55 to tell the teacher she had to make Charles keep quiet, and so Charles had to stay after school. And so all the children stayed to watch him."

"What did he do?" I asked.

"He just sat there," Laurie said, climbing into his chair at the table. "Hi, Pop, y'old dust mop."

60 "Charles had to stay after school today," I told my husband. "Everyone stayed with him."

"What does this Charles look like?" my husband asked Laurie. "What's his other name?"

"He's bigger than me," Laurie said. "And he doesn't have any rubbers
65 and he doesn't ever wear a jacket."

Monday night was the first Parent-Teachers meeting, and only the fact that the baby had a cold kept me from going; I wanted very much to meet Charles's mother. On Tuesday Laurie remarked suddenly, "Our teacher had a friend come to see her in school today."

70 "Charles's mother?" my husband and I asked simultaneously.

"Naaah," Laurie said scornfully. "It was a man who came and made us do exercises, we had to touch our toes. Look." He climbed down from his chair and squatted down and touched his toes. "Like this," he said. He got solemnly back into his chair and said, picking up his fork,
75 "Charles didn't even *do* exercises."

"That's fine," I said heartily. "Didn't Charles want to do exercises?"

"No," Laurie said. "Charles was so fresh to the teacher's friend he wasn't *let* do exercises."

"Fresh again?" I said.

80 "He kicked the teacher's friend," Laurie said. "The teacher's friend told Charles to touch his toes like I just did and Charles kicked him."

"What are they going to do about Charles, do you suppose?" Laurie's father asked him.

Laurie shrugged elaborately. "Throw him out of school, I guess," he said.

85 Wednesday and Thursday were routine; Charles yelled during story hour and hit a boy in the stomach and made him cry. On Friday Charles stayed after school again and so did all the other children.

Threads

Education costs money, but then so does ignorance.

Sir Claus Moser (b. 1922), German-born British academic

Forming Concepts: Thinking about what is going to happen in the story is a good way to understand what you read.

As a class, discuss the following items:

1. Why do you think that all the children stay after school when Charles is bad?
2. Did you have children in your school like Laurie?
3. Did you have children in your school like Charles?

Continue reading:

With the third week of kindergarten Charles was an institution in our family; the baby was being a Charles when she cried all afternoon;
90 Laurie did a Charles when he filled his wagon full of mud and pulled it through the kitchen; even my husband, when he caught his elbow in the telephone cord and pulled telephone, ashtray, and a bowl of flowers off the table, said, after the first minute, "Looks like Charles."

During the third and fourth weeks it looked like a reformation in
95 Charles; Laurie reported grimly at lunch on Thursday of the third week, "Charles was so good today the teacher gave him an apple."

"What?" I said, and my husband added warily, "You mean Charles?"

"Charles," Laurie said. "He gave the crayons around and picked up the books afterward and the teacher said he was her helper."
100 "What happened?" I asked unbelievingly.

"He was her helper, that's all," Laurie said, and shrugged.

"Can this be true, about Charles?" I asked my husband that night. "Can something like this happen?"

"Wait and see," my husband said cynically. "When you've got a Charles
105 to deal with, this may mean he's only plotting."

He seemed to be wrong. For over a week Charles was the teacher's helper; each day he handed things out and he picked things up; no one had to stay after school.

"The P.T.A. meeting's next week again," I told my husband one
110 evening. "I'm going to find Charles's mother there."

"Ask her what happened to Charles," my husband said. "I'd like to know."

"I'd like to know myself," I said.

On Friday of that week things were back to normal. "You know what
115 Charles did today?" Laurie demanded at the dinner table, in a voice slightly awed. "He told a little girl to say a word and she said it and the teacher washed her mouth out with soap and Charles laughed."

"What word?" his father asked unwisely, and Laurie said, "I'll have to
120 whisper it to you, it's so bad." He got down off his chair and went
around to his father. His father bent his head down and Laurie
whispered joyfully. His father's eyes widened.

"Did Charles tell the little girl to say *that?*" he asked respectfully.

"She said it *twice,*" Laurie said. "Charles told her to say it *twice.*"

125 "What happened to Charles?" my husband asked.

"Nothing," Laurie said. "He was passing out the crayons."

Monday morning Charles abandoned the little girl and said the evil
word himself three or four times, getting his mouth washed out with
soap each time. He also threw chalk.

As a class, discuss the following:

1. Why do you think there was a change in Charles' behavior from being
bad to being good?
2. Why do you think Charles' behavior returned to being bad?
3. What do you think about Charles?

Continue reading:

130   My husband came to the door with me that evening as I set out for
the P.T.A. meeting. "Invite her over for a cup of tea after the meeting," he
said. "I want to get a look at her."

"If only she's there," I said prayerfully.

"She'll be there," my husband said. "I don't see how they could hold a
135 P.T.A. meeting without Charles's mother."

At the meeting I sat restlessly, scanning each comfortable matronly
face, trying to determine which one hid the secret of Charles. None of
them looked to me haggard enough. No one stood up in the meeting
and apologized for the way her son had been acting. No one mentioned
140 Charles.

After the meeting I identified and sought out Laurie's kindergarten
teacher. She had a plate with a cup of tea and a piece of marshmellow
cake; I had a plate with a cup of tea and a piece of marshmallow cake.
We maneuvered up to one another cautiously, and smiled.

145   "I've been so anxious to meet you," I said. "I'm Laurie's mother."

"We're all so interested in Laurie," she said.

"Well, he certainly likes kindergarten," I said. "He talks about it all the
time."

"We had a little trouble adjusting, the first week or so," she said
150 primly, "but now he's a fine little helper. With occasional lapses, of
course."

"Laurie usually adjusts very quickly," I said. "I suppose this time it's
Charles's influence."

"Charles?"

155   "Yes," I said, laughing, "you must have your hands full in that
kindergarten, with Charles."

"Charles?" she said. "We don't have any Charles in the kindergarten."

Reading 2: Post-Reading Comprehension Check

Discuss the following question:

1. If there was no Charles, who was Laurie talking about?
2. What do you think the kindergarten teacher was thinking about when she was talking to Laurie's mother?
3. What do you think Laurie's mother was thinking about when she was talking to the kindergarten teacher?
4. Did you expect this outcome in the story? What clues did you have?
5. Have you had a similar experience in school?
6. Have you ever been in trouble at school? What happened? What was your parents' reaction?

READING 3: IN JAPAN, THEIR REASONS ARE MANY

Pre-Reading Discussion

LEARNING STRATEGY

Personalizing: Talking with others before reading helps prepare you for what you will read.

Discuss the following questions:

1. At what age do people usually stop attending school in your country?
2. Are there adult schools in your country? What do adults study?
3. What reasons do adults have for returning to (or staying in) school?
4. What time of day do adult school classes usually meet?

IT WORKS!
Learning Strategy:
Setting a Reading
Rate Goal

In some places in Japan, learning is a continual process. People enroll in classes for self-improvement and enjoyment. Think about this concept in relationship to your experience as you read, *In Japan, Their Reasons Are Many.*

Set a goal for the number of words-per-minute you want to reach while reading. Record that goal here: _____

What is the reading comprehension goal? Record that goal here: _____

Rate Buildup Reading. Remember the directions from earlier. Write the number "1" when the teacher calls out *one minute*. Return to the beginning of the passage and read until the teacher calls *two*. Write the number "2" in the passage. Repeat the sequence a third and fourth time. The goal is to read more text in each minute.

READING 3: IN JAPAN, THEIR REASONS ARE MANY

by Carolyn Andrade

In a country the size of California and with a population more than half as large as the United States, Japan offers many opportunities to learn English. A lot of
5 Japanese speak some English, but many hesitate to admit that they speak it very well. All junior and senior high school students study English at school. Many continue through their university years
10 as well.

For adults who want to learn English, there are abundant opportunities. One way is with a conversation group. These are informal gatherings, usually with a native-
15 English speaker who prepares the topic for the day. Sometimes a conversation group meets in a coffee shop or in someone's home. Another way is to attend classes at a language school. Every large city has
20 several English language schools which operate like businesses. The more students who attend classes, the more money the school makes.

The Komaki English Teaching Center
25 (KETC) is unique among adult programs. Funded by the City of Komaki as a contribution to the internationalization of the regions in and around Komaki City, KETC carries out various educational
30 activities, mainly for Komaki citizens and those who work or study in the city. In addition, KETC plans cultural activities for students, their families, and for the community at large. Such activities include:
35 American Movie Nights, Monopoly Nights, Family Picnics, an English Language Fair, and various holiday parties.

Among KETC adult students, their reasons for learning English are as varied as
40 their numbers. Many people want to travel to English-speaking countries such as Australia, New Zealand, Canada or America. Some people want to be able to socialize with foreigners who visit Japan.

45 Others find English useful in their jobs. Masuko Suzuki works for a large Japanese company which has several international offices. She often translates faxes or answers telephone calls from abroad. Takeshi Ogawa
50 works for another large Japanese company. He is learning English so he can be transferred to the American office someday.

Atsuko Takeda and Yukiko Yamada are housewives and mothers. They study English
55 so that they can help their junior high school-aged children with their homework. Kiyoko Tanaka is also a housewife. She is an expert in performing the Japanese Tea Ceremony. Someday she wants to share this
60 ancient Japanese tradition with English-speaking people around the world.

Many Japanese enjoy watching American movies. Keiko Matsumoto has to read the Japanese subtitles now. She
65 studies English so that she will be able to understand the dialogue of American movies.

Fifteen years ago when Naoyuki Inagaki graduated from the university, he lived in
70 America for over a year. He also traveled a lot. He saw the Statue of Liberty in New York, Mt. Rushmore in South Dakota and the Grand Canyon in Arizona. His English is excellent. Although he only occasionally
75 uses English at work, he studies English so he won't forget it.

It is difficult to generalize about why Japanese study English. KETC students and students throughout Japan study English for
80 many different reasons.

IT WORKS!
Learning Strategy:
Evaluating Your
Reading Rate

Evaluate your reading rate performance.

1. How many lines of text did you read the first time? Write the number here: _____

2. Multiply the number of lines you read in the first one-minute segment by 7. Write the product here: _____ (This is approximately the number of words that you read the first minute.)

3. How many lines of text did you read the fourth time? Write the number here: _____

4. Multiply the number of lines you read the fourth one-minute segment by 7. Write the product here: _____ (This is approximately the number of words that you read the fourth minute.)

5. What was your reading rate goal? Write your goal here: _____

6. Compare the numbers in #2 and #4 with your goal in #5. How well did you do in accomplishing your reading rate goal?

Threads

What does education often do? It makes a straight-cut ditch of a free, meandering brook.

Henry David Thoreau
(1817–1962), U.S. philosopher,
author, naturalist

Scan the passage, *In Japan, Their Reasons Are Many,* to find the answers to the following questions.

1. What is the population comparison made between the U.S. and Japan?

    _____

2. Where is one place that a conversation group might meet?

    _____

3. List some of the activities that KETC offers students.

    _____

    _____

4. Why is Masuko Suzuki studying English?

    _____

5. Why is Naoyuki Inagaki studying English?

    _____

IT WORKS!
Learning Strategy:
Scanning for
Specific
Information

Reading 3: Post-Reading Comprehension Check

LEARNING STRATEGY

Remembering New Material: Trying to remember what you understand from a reading helps you develop better comprehension skills

Write short answers to the following questions. Then share your responses with a classmate.

1. Why is KETC unique among adult language programs?

    _____

    _____

2. What are some of the reasons that KETC students give for studying English?

    _____

    _____

3. Why would someone study English to watch American movies?

_____

_____

4. Do you know people who have similar reasons for studying English as the students at KETC?

_____

_____

5. Why are you studying English?

_____

_____

LEARNING STRATEGY

Personalizing: Relating what you read to your previous personal experience improves your comprehension.

READING 4: LEARNING TO READ IN ARGENTINA AND MALAYSIA

Pre-Reading Discussion

*IT WORKS!
Learning Strategy:
Setting a Reading
Rate Goal*

Discuss the following questions as a class.

1. Are there schools in your home country, or in the area that you live in now, that have a good reputation for high educational standards?

2. Are there schools in your home country, or in the area that you live in now, that have a bad reputation for high educational standards?

3. What makes these schools strong or weak?

4. Where does strong education begin? Why do you feel that way?

5. If parents are involved in the schools, does that strengthen the educational program? Why? Why not?

Set a goal for the number of words-per-minute you want to reach while reading *Learning to Read in Argentina and Malaysia.*

Record that goal here: _____

What is the reading comprehension goal?

Record that goal here: _____

READING 4: LEARNING TO READ IN ARGENTINA AND MALAYSIA

by Ana Paulina Peña Pollastri and Lee Ng

Learning to read can be exciting for a child. Exposure to books, magazines, and newspapers gives a reader a new view of the world. Many wonderful things can be

5 learned while reading. Reading serves many purposes as well. Some people read to get information while others read for entertainment. Once a child has unlocked the door to reading, much information can

10 be received. Many consider reading to be the cornerstone of learning.

The methods for teaching children how to read can be different from one country to another. These methods can even be

15 different within the same country. Some reading methods focus the reader first on the sound system of the language while others begin by focusing on the message. Two examples of the different methods of

20 teaching children to read can be found from experiences of learners from Argentina and Malaysia.

ARGENTINA

In the city of La Rioja, Argentina, Father

25 Blecker teaches at the *Colegio del Sagrado Corazon de Jesus.* His method resembles "conventional reading instruction" by starting with sounds of the alphabet and building to syllables, words then sentences.

30 The unique thing about the Blecker method is that it is designed so that each letter is represented by a picture of an object that begins with the letter and that resembles it in shape. For example, the letter *u* is known

35 as *uña* (fingernail) and the picture of the word is a fingernail pointing downwards.

Father Blecker's alphabet even addresses a phonological peculiarity of Spanish. There is a different pronunciation of the letters *c*

40 and *g* in the syllables *ca, co, cu* (pronounced /ka/, /ko/, /ku/) and *ga, go, gu* (pronounced ga, go, gu) as opposed to the syllables *ce, ci*

(pronounced /say/, /see/) and *ge, gi,* (pronounced /shey/, /she/). The method

45 provides key words with these sounds at the beginning of words in Spanish. The aim of the alphabet is to help young learners memorize a set of words whose shape is associated with pronunciation and meaning

50 rather than on isolated sounds.

Paulina Peña remembers learning to read using the Blecker method. She recalls that Father Blecker departed from traditional "rules" in the classroom to encourage

55 reading. Instead of having his students seated in rows in the classroom, he encouraged students to sing songs and play games. The songs and games matched the alphabet system. His classes were always

60 shifting from reading to singing or playing in the classroom. Father Blecker did not confine students to a textbook. He displayed a wide variety of hand-written and printed material in the classroom for the students.

65 He empowered the students to recognize the same letter in a variety of settings and styles.

The *Blecker System* proved to be very effective for Paulina. After a two-month

70 period of instruction, she was able to read, though haltingly, any kind of printed material she was exposed to. She went from reading the Grimm fairy tale *Little Red Ridinghood* to Alcott's *Little Women* and

75 Tolstoi's *War and Peace.*

MALAYSIA

Many children in Malaysia learn to read in more than one language. Lee Ng is one such learner. She reads Mandarin, English,

80 and Malay. She learned how to read in Mandarin before she was in kindergarten. She learned to read Mandarin by listening to her mother read stories from the Sunday newspaper. This weekly routine consisted of

Lee's mother picking out the children's section and narrating a story to her. She always looked forward to the storytelling sessions because she liked to look at the colorful pictures and listen to her mother's narration.

The stories were usually presented in a progression of colorful illustrations with words printed at the bottom of every picture. Lee's mother would answer her questions and allow her to create her own endings to the folk tales. As she grew older, Lee looked forward to the stories published in the newspaper. The discovery of the weekly children's section encouraged her to learn to read Chinese. Lee did not want to have to depend on adults to tell her the stories. This motivated her to learn.

Lee started learning the Roman alphabet only when she was in kindergarten. It was not very interesting to her at first. The lessons focused mostly on individual words and not on stories. However, she was a great fan of English cartoons, so the need to find out the airtime of cartoons on television necessitated learning to read the TV guide. Often there were changes in the airtime for the cartoons. Lee found that her father's English newspaper was one source with the most up-to-date information of the program summaries. She learned to read the summaries of the programs that were in the newspaper and then continued her reading experience with books in English.

The reading skill in Malay was the only skill that Lee started learning through formal schooling when she was around nine or ten years old. The reason she never pushed herself to read earlier in Malay was because she did not have a need to learn to read that language. The people she came in contact with were mostly Chinese. Lee's reading skills in Malay improved tremendously when the TV station in Malaysia started dubbing Japanese TV programs into the Malay language. Lee had a need to learn to read because the television subtitles for these Japanese TV programs were in Malay. She suddenly had a reason to read Malay so that she could get the meaning of the Japanese television programs.

Both Paulina and Lee learned to read through different methods. Paulina's teacher focused on learning the alphabet in Spanish and using the sounds to learn words and meaning. Lee focused on meaning then learned to read the words. These are different ways of learning to read. Both women have become very proficient readers in more than one language.

We learn faster when we can read. It isn't important what method was used to teach us how to read. What is important is that we read and continue to learn.

Record your reading rate on the rate chart in Appendix B.

Reading 4: Post-Reading Comprehension Check

Without looking back at the passage, complete the following comprehension statements/questions by circling the appropriate letter.

1. One main idea from this passage is that
   a. students in Argentina learn how to read early in school.
   b. reading is an important part of learning new information.
   c. watching television supports your reading development.
   d. the method for teaching reading should be the same for everyone.

2. The article talks about two methods of teaching reading.
   One focuses on the sounds of a language while the other
   a. focuses on the message of the reading.
   b. teaches children to read in more than one language.
   c. focuses on pictures based on the sounds.
   d. teaches readers from different countries.

3. The reading system developed by Father Blecker advances from sounds to
   a. meaning, pictures, then stories.
   b. pictures then sentences.
   c. syllables, words, then sentences.
   d. sentences through pictures.

4. Spanish has a unique feature for some letters of the alphabet. The pronunciation of
   a. *c* and *g* are the same when followed by certain vowel sounds.
   b. vowel sound changes if a word begins with *c* or *g*.
   c. key words change because of the letters *c* and *g*.
   d. *c* and *g* change depending on the vowel that comes after.

5. The purpose of Father Blecker's alphabet is to
   a. learn pronunciation and meaning rather than single sounds.
   b. learn to sing and have fun in the classroom.
   c. teach students to read in a very short time.
   d. follow classroom rules as you learn to read.

6. Seeing a letter in many different words is important for learning because
   a. they are included in many textbooks.
   b. songs and games can match letters.
   c. we can then read only fairy tales.
   d. we can then read a wide variety of material.

7. In the story, Lee learned to read Mandarin by

    a. learning a picture for sounds in the language.

    b. watching television and repeating what she heard.

    c. listening to her mother read stories to her.

    d. reading the newspaper for summaries of articles.

8. Lee learned to read in three languages. One thing that was the same in learning in all three languages was

    a. getting the message from the printed material.

    b. listening to her mother read to her.

    c. watching cartoons or movies on television.

    d. reading newspapers and watching television.

9. Lee made improvement in her ability to read Malay when she began

    a. reading the newspaper for reviews of television programs.

    b. listening to cartoons and seeing the action on television.

    c. listening to her mother describe pictures from the newspaper.

    d. reading the subtitles of foreign television programs.

10. An important idea suggested by the authors is that we learn faster when

    a. we are taught with a special method.

    b. we can read and continue learning.

    c. we read in more than one language.

    d. we learn the alphabet first.

IT WORKS!
Learning Strategy:
Dare to Dream

Total number of correct answers: _____ / 10

Record your reading comprehension score on the comprehension chart in Appendix C.

READING STRATEGY CHECKLIST

Check off the strategies you used while reading the passage and answering the questions.

_____ I created a mental picture of what I was reading.

_____ I guessed the meaning of words I did not know.

_____ I translated some vocabulary and ideas from my native language into English.

_____ I asked myself questions while I was reading to check my own comprehension.

_____ Others? Write them here: _____

_____

_____

Managing Your Learning: Evaluating your reading performance helps you improve it.

Record your reading rate on the graph in Appendix B. How does your reading rate on this passage compare with your rate on the other passages? Slower? Faster? The same?

Did you reach the reading rate goal you set before reading?

Each of the comprehension questions above can be classified into one of three reading comprehension categories:

• Understanding Main Ideas,
• Understanding Direct Statements, or
• Understanding Inferences.

Review your performance on each question and record your performance on the chart provided in Appendix C. How does your reading comprehension on this passage compare with the previous passages? Lower? Higher? The same?

Did you reach the reading comprehension goal you set before reading?

After checking your answers, get into groups of three and compare your answers. Find evidence from the reading to support your answers.

POST-READING EVALUATION

Respond in writing to the following questions, then discuss your answers with others in your class.

1 What have you learned from all the readings in this chapter on education?

_____

_____

_____

_____

2. How has your knowledge changed as a result of these readings?

_____

_____

_____

_____

IT WORKS!
Learning Strategy:
Evaluating What
You Have Learned

3. How has your attitude about national education standards changed as a result of these readings?

_____

_____

_____

_____

4. What can you do to show that you are more aware of educational goals for yourself and education systems at the local and national level?

_____

_____

_____

_____

5. Which reading goals did you achieve in this chater?

_____

_____

6. What will be your primary goal in the next chapter?

_____

_____

Understanding Time: Are You Using It Wisely?

 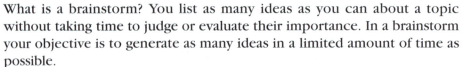

What is a brainstorm? You list as many ideas as you can about a topic without taking time to judge or evaluate their importance. In a brainstorm your objective is to generate as many ideas in a limited amount of time as possible.

Your brainstorm task for this chapter is to list as many ideas and/or questions as you can about the concept of TIME. Your teacher will give you five minutes to brainstorm.

_____

_____

_____

_____

_____

_____

Threads

Time: That which man is always trying to kill, but which ends in killing him.

Herbert Spencer

_____

_____

_____

_____

_____

_____

_____

_____

_____

_____

_____

_____

_____

With your list of ideas and/or questions from your brainstorm, meet with a partner and share your lists. Together generate a new list of at least five ideas and/or and questions you would like to share with the class.

1. _____
   _____

2. _____
   _____

3. _____
   _____

4. _____
   _____

5. _____
   _____

READING 1: HOW WINDUP ALARM CLOCKS WORK

Pre-Reading Discussion

VISUALIZING THE INSIDE OF A WINDUP CLOCK

Discuss the following questions as a class or with a partner:

1. What kind of an alarm clock do you use?
2. What are the advantages of a windup alarm clock as opposed to an electric alarm clock?
3. What does the inside of a windup alarm clock look like? Form a mental image of the inside of a windup alarm clock.

IT WORKS!
Learning Strategy:
Using Imagery

Based on the mental image you have formed in question #3 above, try to draw a picture of what you see in your mind.

Compare your drawing with that of a partner in your class. What similarities do you see? What differences do you see? Compare your drawing and your partner's drawing with the drawing that accompanies the next reading passage entitled, "How Windup Alarm Clocks Work." What characteristics of your drawing are part of the drawing which accompanies the reading passage? What similarities and differences do you see?

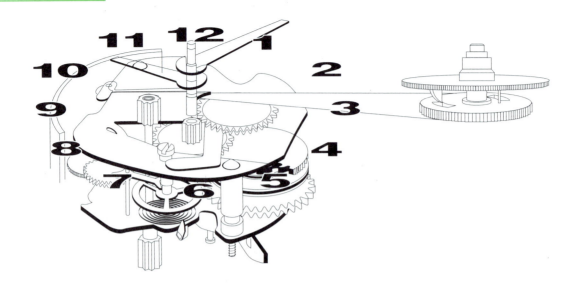

LEARNING STRATEGY

Managing Your Learning: Setting goals for your reading rate helps you improve it.

What is the overall reading rate goal you would like to work towards in this chapter? Record that goal here: _____

What is the overall reading comprehension goal you would like to work towards in this chapter? Record that goal here: _____

Reading Skill Improvement

READING RATE INSTRUCTION

Rate Buildup Reading. Read for four 60-second periods. Each time the teacher calls out the number (1, 2, 3, or 4) write it in the text where you are. The purpose of this activity is to reread *old* material quickly, gliding into the new. As your eyes move quickly over the *old* material you will learn how to get your eyes moving at a faster reading rate. This exercise involves more than simply moving your eyes quickly, you should understand what you are reading. As you participate in this rate building activity, you will learn to increase your reading rate.

READING 1: HOW WINDUP ALARM CLOCKS WORK

by Marvin J. Fryer

You may have an electric clock-radio that wakes you to music, or you may use a simple windup alarm clock. The power for windup alarms comes from a metal coil inside the
5 clock called a mainspring. You wind the mainspring by turning a key. As the spring unwinds, it supplies power to move the hands.

How does the mainspring do this?
10 Inside, the clock has a series of large and small wheels with toothed edges. The mainspring is attached to a large wheel called the main wheel. As the mainspring unwinds, the main wheel turns with it. The
15 teeth of the main wheel mesh with the teeth of the next wheel in the series. All the wheels fit together in this way. As the main wheel turns, each wheel turns the wheel next to it.

20 Wheels of different sizes take different amounts of time to make a full revolution. The wheels are arranged so that the hour hand and the minute hand turn at different speeds to keep the right time. The whole
25 series of moving wheels is called the wheel train. Without something to stop it, the mainspring would unwind as soon as you finished winding it. A mechanism called the escapement acts as a brake. It keeps the
30 power of the mainspring from "escaping." The escapement consists of three parts: a balance wheel, a tiny metal spring called a hairspring, and a lever. The hairspring controls the motion of the balance wheel.
35 When the balance wheel turns one way, the hairspring tightens. Then the hairspring unwinds, pushing the balance wheel back the other way. That makes the balance wheel rock to and fro. As the balance
40 wheel rocks, it pushes the lever back and forth. When the lever moves, two pins on the end of the lever take turns catching the teeth of the adjoining wheel. This wheel is connected to the last wheel of the wheel
45 train and slows down the whole wheel train by making it stop and go. You hear this action as the tick-tock tick-tock in your clock.

Managing Your Learning: Evaluating your reading rate helps you focus on your progress.

Evaluate your reading rate performance.

1. How many lines of text did you read the first time? Write the number here: _____

2. Multiply the number of lines you read the first one-minute segment by 8. Write the product here: _____ (This is approximately the number of words that you read the first minute.)

3. How many lines of text did you read the fourth time? Write the number here: _____

4. Multiply the number of lines you read the fourth one-minute segment by 8. Write the product here: _____ (This is approximately the number of words that you read the fourth minute.)

5. What was your reading rate goal? Write your goal here: _____

6. Compare the numbers in #2 and #4 above with your goal in #5. How well did you do in accomplishing your reading rate goal?

Threads

Time and I against any two.

Spanish proverb

Reading 1: Post-Reading Comprehension Check

Forming Concepts: Distinguishing the main ideas from supporting ideas and details helps you better comprehend the entire reading.

Below, is a list of eight sentences from the passage *How Windup Alarm Clocks Work*. Put each sentence into a category by placing the appropriate letter in the blank before the sentence—Main ideas (M), Supporting ideas (S), or Details (D).

_____ 1. As the spring unwinds, it supplies power to move the hands.

_____ 2. You may have an electric clock-radio that wakes you to music, or you may use a simpler windup alarm clock.

_____ 3. The power for windup alarms comes from a metal coil inside the clock called a mainspring.

_____ 4. When the lever moves, two pins on the end of the lever take turns catching the teeth of the adjoining wheel.

___ **5.** A mechanism called the escapement acts as a brake. It keeps the power of the mainspring from "escaping."

___ **6.** You hear this action as the tick-tock tick-tock in your clock.

___ **7.** Without something to stop it, the mainspring would unwind as soon as you finished winding it.

___ **8.** The main-spring is attached to a large wheel called the main wheel.

Compare your list with a partner in class. Then discuss what you learned about windup alarm clocks.

LEARNING STRATEGY

Overcoming Limitations: Comparing your work with a model often helps you overcome limitations.

Compare your list with the classification below of main ideas, supporting ideas, and details. Discuss the list as a class.

MAIN IDEAS	SUPPORTING IDEAS	DETAILS
3	1	2
7	5	4
		6
		8

READING 2: STANDARDIZING TIME

Pre-Reading Discussion

In the next reading passage you will have an opportunity to work alone as well as with a small group of your peers. Monitor your feelings to see in which mode you feel most comfortable.

IT WORKS!
Learning Strategy:
Cooperating with
Peers

LEARNING STRATEGY

Managing Your Learning: Overviewing and linking with already known material helps you understand new material.

WORD SEARCH

Hidden in the grid below are vocabulary words from the upcoming reading selection, *Standardizing Time*. The words can occur forward, backward, horizontally, vertically, or diagonally. A list of all the hidden words in the word search are listed below. After you find each word, circle it and cross it off the list. One word has already been completed for you.

~~ante~~	lunar	pole	solar
continuous	meridian	post	zones
degrees	midnight	prime	

```
B  T  F  O  I  B  J  H  U  P  N  E
J  F  C  M  Z  T  T  C  D  O  I  P
S  X  Y  R  I  W  A  O  W  S  E  R
O  O  S  M  X  D  T  N  Z  T  K  I
L  X  Y  N  E  W  N  T  T  C  N  M
A  R  M  W  V  U  F  I  L  E  G  E
R  A  E  X  D  Z  W  N  G  I  C  A
U  N  R  Z  E  A  M  U  D  H  M  P
R  U  I  O  G  Z  V  O  X  E  T  O
U  L  D  N  R  Q  S  U  O  B  T  L
E  M  I  E  E  N  E  S  Q  Z  Y  E
H  K  A  S  E  X  T  S  M  O  Z  C
W  F  N  L  S  B  G  L  K  N  B  H
```

Working with a small group of students in your class, see if you know the meanings of the words from the word search. If you do not know, ask other students in your group, your teacher, or look up the word in a dictionary. Make a list of the words you do not know and write a brief definition below.

1. _____

2. _____

3. _____

4. _____

5. _____

6. _____

7. _____

Review the vocabulary prior to reading the next passage, *Standardizing Time.*

Look at the drawing. What do you know about time zones in the world? Using the vocabulary learned previously and from this drawing, make a list of five things you already know about time zones in the world.

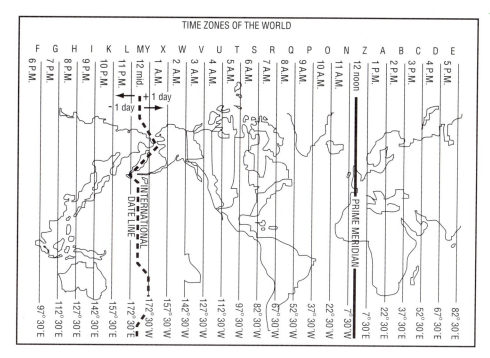

1. _____

2. _____

3. _____

4. _____

5. _____

Do you like working alone or with others? In what settings do you learn best alone? In what settings do you learn best with others? Knowing what works well for you is an important part of learning.

Reading Skill Improvement

READING RATE INSTRUCTION

Class-paced reading. For this reading passage we are going to read the passage at a minimal reading rate of 150 words-per-minute. As you read the following passage on standardizing time, the teacher will call out the numbers one through four. Each time the teacher calls out a number you should be near the same bold-faced number that is in the margin. If you are not at the bold-faced number when the teacher calls it, skip from where you are currently reading to the number. Do everything you can to keep up with the minimal reading rate of 150 words-per-minute.

If you pass a bold-faced number before the teacher calls it, keep reading. You are reading faster than 150 words-per-minute. As long as you are keeping up with the numbers the teacher calls out, you are reading at the minimal reading rate goal.

READING 2: STANDARDIZING TIME

by Beulah Tannenbaum and Myra Stillman

Time is like a continuous line which has no obvious beginning nor end. For example, when did today begin? In most countries of the world, the answer is at midnight, but this was
5 not always the case. Probably the rising Sun was used by earliest man to indicate the beginning of a new day. Egypt and, later, Rome, both of which used solar midnight, began the day at sunrise. Because Babylonia and Biblical
10 Israel had lunar calendars, they were more concerned with nighttime, and therefore dated the new day at sundown.

Since the time when the Sun rises and sets changes daily, this system would be confusing
15 in our complicated modern world. It is simplest to change dates at midnight. But until man had invented an accurate way to measure the hours of the night it was necessary to use the Sun to mark the coming of a new day.   **1**

20   The circumference of the Earth is a circle, and therefore can be divided into 360 degrees. It takes twenty-four hours for the Earth to spin around. In 1884, the representatives of many governments held an
25 international conference in Washington, D.C., and approved a plan to divide the entire world into twenty-four time zones, each fifteen degrees in width. Each of these time zones extends from the North Pole to the South Pole.

30   Each of the lines separating the time zones is a meridian. A meridian is one half of a great circle on the globe which passes from Pole to Pole. The abbreviation A.M., for ante meridian, comes from the Latin and means "before the
35 meridian," or "before noon." P.M., or post meridian, is also Latin and means "after the meridian," or "afternoon."

Meridians are numbered in degrees east and west of the prime meridian. At the 1884 **2**
40 Washington Conference, it was agreed that the meridian passing through the Greenwich Observatory in London, England, would be called the prime meridian.

45   The Greenwich Civil Time Zone (G.C.T.) extends 7 1/2 degrees east and 7 1/2 degrees west of the prime meridian. The time zone directly west of the Greenwich Zone covers the 15 degrees from 7 1/2 degrees West to 22
50 1/2 degrees West. When it is 12, noon, at Greenwich, it is one hour earlier, or 11 A.M., in the meridian to the west. A man traveling west from Greenwich must set his watch back one hour as he crosses into each new time zone.

55   When it is 12, noon, at Greenwich, it is one hour later, or 1 P.M., in the time zone immediately east. A man traveling east from Greenwich must set his watch ahead one hour as he crosses into each new time zone.   **3**

60   Although the Washington Conference divided the world into 15-degree sections, a glance at the time zone map will show you that zone lines do not follow meridian lines exactly. Smaller countries and states find it less
65 confusing to be entirely within one time zone. So the lines are twisted to follow political boundaries. Some American towns, such as Apalachicola, Florida; Stockton, Kansas; and Huntington, Oregon; are located on time zone
70 lines. In these cases, the lines are bent around the town so that the people will not lose or gain an hour whenever they go from one side of the town to the other.

Keeping track of time in different parts of
75 the world is certainly easier today due to the standardization of time zones. The ever moving aspect of time seems to be more manageable within this system. Einstein once summed up the continuity of time in   **4**
80 a clever joke. Closing the door behind a guest who had overstayed his welcome, the great scientist remarked that "time is like a departing guest, always going, but never gone!"

How well did you do in this minimal reading rate activity? Choose the description below that best describes your reading performance.

1. I was able to keep up at 150 words-per-minute.
2. I read faster than 150 words-per-minute.
3. I was reading slower than 150 words-per-minute.

Reading 2: Post-Reading Comprehension Check

Based on the text in *Standardizing Time,* write a summary of the most important ideas. Topic sentences usually reflect the most important information. Rewrite the topic sentences in your own words. Write your summary below.

_____

_____

_____

_____

_____

_____

_____

Compare your summary with the summary of a classmate. What elements in your summary are part of your partner's summary? What elements of your partner's summary are not included in your summary? Then, compare your summary with the summary below. How are the summaries you and your partner wrote similar to or different from the one below?

In evaluating the strength of a summary you should consider the following factors: (1) What were the main ideas of the reading passage? (2) Did I include those ideas in my summary? (3) What were the supporting ideas of the reading passage? (4) Did I include supporting ideas in my summary? (5) What were the details of the reading passage? (6) Did I include details in my summary? (7) Did I use my own words?

SUMMARY OF STANDARDIZING TIME

Time has no beginning or end. Each new day begins at midnight according to our clocks. In earlier times, the day began at sunrise, but since the time of sunrise changes every day that is not a good system to use today. The world is divided into twenty-four time zones. Each dividing line is a meridian. A.M. means before the meridian (ante) and P.M. means after the meridian (post). The prime meridian passes through the Greenwich Observatory in London, England. Each time zone covers 15 degrees of the earth's circumference. The time zone lines are not straight, but are adjusted to fit political boundaries. Because keeping track of time is now standard in the world it seems easier to manage.

Discuss these ideas as a class.

Pre-Reading Discussion

As you read the next passage, in addition to developing a reading rate of 150 wpm, think about how you use your time. If you have some "empty time" do you feel anxious? Do you feel happy? Do you know people who are "scared" when they have an empty hour? What do you do with your "empty" time?

IT WORKS!
Learning Strategy:
Taking Your
Emotional
Temperature

Reading Skill Improvement

READING RATE INSTRUCTION

Class paced reading. Let's read a second passage at a minimal reading rate of 150 words-per-minute. As you read the following passage entitled, *Why an Empty Hour Scares Us,* the teacher will call out the numbers one through four. Each time the teacher calls out a number you should be near the same bold-faced number in the margin. If you are not at the bold-faced number when the teacher calls it, skip from where you are currently reading to the number. Do everything you can to keep up with the minimal reading rate of 150 words-per-minute.

If you pass a bold-faced number before the teacher calls it, keep reading. You are reading faster than 150 words-per-minute. As long as you are keeping up with the numbers the teacher calls out, you are reading at the minimal reading rate goal.

READING 3: WHY AN EMPTY HOUR SCARES US

by Stephan Rechtschaffen

There are cultures on this planet that have no word for minute or hour, cultures where a moment can last a whole morning. We don't live in one of them. In the western
5 culture the efficient and productive use of time has become high art. If you can manage your time well, you are often given more things to do.

A curious thing happens as the pace of
10 our lives grows faster and faster: Our definition of a "moment" grows shorter and shorter, moving our awareness of time into smaller increments. By filling each moment so full of events, we leave ourselves no time
15 to actually experience these events in any meaningful way.

As a result, the future arrives that much quicker, and it begins to dominate. The "now" becomes a prelude for the "next."
20 We finish this so we can get to that. We work for the weekend, rush through lunch to get back to our desks, and worry about next month's deadline before this month is complete. We are so focused on what's
25 ahead that we just can't come alive in the here and now.

The pace of our lives has created a chasm between our emotions and our thoughts, which operate at different speeds.
30 Thoughts are processed electrically, communicating faster than our emotions, which are hormonal and chemical. The demands of the modern world have required us to function more quickly, so we use what
35 I call "mind time" to mentally engage to our fullest in order to juggle upcoming events. There is no time to deal with or process our slower feelings—utilizing what I call "emotional time"—so we repress them or
40 stuff them down.

But our emotions don't disappear, nor do they stay down

for long. The moment we begin to slow **2** down, they come flooding back in and we
45 begin to feel again. Unfortunately, many people report that when they try to relax, what comes up are uncomfortable emotions—anxiety or anger over unresolved encounters, guilt over inactivity. So we get
50 busy again, and repress once more those feelings that allow us to fully experience our lives. If our experience of slowing down is always pain or discomfort, no wonder we can't sit still, no wonder we busy ourselves
55 and continue to feel in a rush to accomplish.

What we need is to come into the present moment. Instead of rushing, take your time, let your rhythm slow down. You can rush later if you need to, but for now,
60 simply perform the task that is in front of you, whether it's washing the dishes or commuting to work.

We spend our lives waiting for the important events to take place, rushing **3**
65 through all these "in-between" moments. Yet the reality is that these interims actually make up a significant portion of our lives. Allowing ourselves to be present in them and experience them fully is what makes us
70 alive. This involves developing a sense of mindfulness, a way of being that puts you fully in the moment without pressure or anxiety about staying on schedule.

The key is to step back from the edge,
75 to learn to get involved in the process rather than constantly longing for the end result. This does not mean giving up our goal-oriented lives, but simply modifying them, finding a balance between our productive
80 and our emotional selves. **3.45**

1 *(margin marker at line 21)*

How well did you do in this minimal reading rate activity? Choose the description below that best describes your reading performance.

1. I was able to keep up at 150 words-per-minute.
2. I read faster than 150 words-per-minute.
3. I was reading slower than 150 words-per-minute.

IT WORKS!
Learning Strategy:
Evaluating Your
Reading Rate

Reading 3: Post-Reading Comprehension Check

With a partner, discuss the following questions:

IT WORKS!
Learning Strategy:
Evaluating Your
Emotional
Temperature

1. What is the significance of the title of this reading, *Why an Empty Hour Scares Us*?
2. Are you ever "scared" to have an empty hour?
3. Do you know people who are scared when they have some unexpected free time?
4. What advice does the author of this article give to someone who is scared of an empty hour?

READING 4: THE TIME OF OUR LIVES

Pre-Reading Discussion

In American English many idiomatic expressions are used that refer to the element of TIME. Discuss with a partner as many expressions as you can think of, in English or translations from your own language, which deal with the concept of TIME. Write your expressions below.

_____

_____

_____

_____

_____

_____

_____

_____

Compare your findings with the following idiomatic expressions. Discuss these expressions with each other. What do these idiomatic expressions about *time* mean? Did you and your partner identify expressions that are not included in the list below?

Time waits for no one.
Don't waste your time.
You can kill time.
Time is money.
Time marches on.
His love failed the test of time.
She is precise as clockwork.
Let's beat the clock.
I had the time of my life.
That movie is timeless.
Time flies when you're having fun.
He is living on borrowed time.
Giving gifts is a time-honored tradition.
She has too much time on her hands.
Time doesn't stand still.
We can save time by doing it my way.
There is no time like the present.
Ahead of / behind the times.
I lost track of the time.
What is the timeframe for completing the work?

Threads

O, for an engine to keep
back all clocks.

Ben Johnson

The next reading passage is called *The Time of Our Lives*. The reading incorporates some of the idiomatic expressions discussed in it as the author discusses the role of time in our lives.

As you read, your teacher will time your reading. When you complete the reading passage, look up at your teacher and record your reading time.

Set a goal for the number of words-per-minute you want to reach while reading *The Time Of Our Lives*.

*IT WORKS!
Learning Strategy:
Setting a Reading
Rate Goal*

Record that goal here: _____

What is your reading comprehension goal?

Record that goal here: _____

READING 4: THE TIME OF OUR LIVES

by Don Dedera

American baseball player Yogi Berra has proclaimed, "Time is what keeps everything from happening all at once." Of all that has been said about time, that remark might be
5 the most sensible. Even Albert Einstein was at a loss for words to explain time, and he was the one who first thought of it as a physical dimension.

Writer John Boslough in *National*
10 *Geographic* has quoted Nobel laureate Richard P. Feynman: "We physicists work with [time] every day, but don't ask me what it is. It's just too difficult to think about." He echoes St. Augustine of 15 centuries ago:
15 "What then is time? If someone asks me. I know. If I wish to explain it to someone who asks, I know not."

Time is money, goes a business-world saying—that is, of material value. Although
20 time cannot be deposited in a bank, some people are said to be living on borrowed time. We kill it, save it, waste it. One behavior may be time-honored, while another fails the test of it. With time on your
25 hands, can you suffer the ravages of it? Most Americans think of time as a straight, steady line of connected intervals. Yet when lovers are together, time flies, and when they are apart, it crawls.

30 From the beginning, humankind has done a better job of measuring time than explaining it. Students of ancient history speculate that the seasons, ranging from two (wet and dry) in equatorial Africa to as many
35 as six for North American Indian tribes, were the only subdivisions meaningful to hunters, gatherers and early farmers. And that before the coming of artificial light, smaller measurements were applied only to
40 daytime.

Celestial movements suggest useful time frames: one spin of Earth, a day; the moon's comings and goings, a month; Earth's orbit around the sun, a year. But the week seems
45 to have been a practical, human invention.

Greeks and Romans developed the sundial, with which they divided daylight into 12 portions. With this system, summer's dozen hours were much longer than
50 winter's. These timepieces were useful but they worked decreasingly well when removed from the equator, and did not work at all when the sun wasn't shining. To augment and replace sun time, the Chinese,
55 Syrians and other peoples for 500 years devised numerous diverse and ingenious water clocks. The passage of fluid in and out of vessels more or less could be controlled and given value.

60 Regardless of which method of measurements were used, be they sandglasses, notched candles, oil burners or incense sticks, length of hours varied with seasonal periods of light and dark. Not until
65 the appearance of mechanical clocks in the 13th century did the idea of 24 equal-time hours gain wide acceptance. The partition of an hour into 60 minutes and a minute into 60 seconds is an arbitrary decision traced
70 back through Egypt and Babylon to Greece.

The name is lost of the genius who invented the mechanical clock. This unknown wizard determined that the energy reposing in a hanging weight could be
75 released intermittently and regularly through an action called escapement. The key was an adjustable, rocking horizontal bar that divided power into periods of time. Then, through cogged wheels and other devices,
80 the clock struck 24 equal-length hours. Most time experts conclude that time is infinitely divisible, limited only by our technology.

In terms of measuring time, the human race has done very well. But in terms of

85 making the best use of it we still have much to learn.

In the *Joy of Working,* Denis Waitley reasons, "Time is an equal opportunity employer. Each human being has exactly the 90 same number of hours and minutes every day. Rich people can't buy more hours. Scientists can't invent new minutes. And you can't save time to spend it on another day. Even so, time is amazingly fair and forgiving. 95 No matter how much time you've wasted in the past, you have an entire tomorrow. Success depends upon using it wisely—by planning and setting priorities. The fact is, time is worth more than money, and by 100 killing time, we are killing our own chances for success."

Perhaps the best-known proof of the theory occurred a century ago in the business life of steel magnate Andrew 105 Carnegie. Complaining that he couldn't get anything done, he called in an authority in time management, who told him, "I'll give you the secret. Use it for 30 days. If it works, you must pay me $25,000. If is doesn't work, 110 you owe me nothing."

At the end of the month, Carnegie again summoned the advisor. He handed over the money. The secret: "Start each day with a list of things to do. Put first the most important.

115 Work hard on that project. If by the end of the day you accomplish nothing else, you will have furthered your most important task."

For our day, the most widely read time-120 management expert has been Alan Lakein. Over the past two decades, his book *How to Get Control of Your Time and Your Life* has sold countless copies. Lakein's system likewise employs a "To Do" list, but he is not 125 an "efficiency expert" or "time-and-motion organizer." Instead, Lakein challenges readers to write down their life goals. Then, from self-rated lists, readers are encouraged to do the important things first. Lakein 130 refuses to buy the oft-heard complaint that there simply are not enough hours in the day.

He lectures, "Time is life. It is irreversible and irreplaceable. To waste your 135 time is to waste your life, but to master your time is to master your life and make the most of it."

As Gernot Winkler, director of the Time Service Department at the U.S. Naval 140 Observatory in Washington, D.C., once put it: "We have given more attention to measuring time than [any other variable] in nature. But time remains an abstraction, a riddle that exists only in our minds."

Record your reading rate on the rate chart in Appendix B.

Reading 4: Post-Reading Comprehension Check

Without looking back at the passage *The Time of Our Lives,* complete the
statements or answer the questions by circling the correct letter.

1. One of the main points the writer is making is that
   a. time management advice is worth $25,000 when used for a period
      of 30 days.
   b. mechanical clocks are much better than sundials, sandglasses, or
      water clocks.
   c. even with all the attention given to measuring time, it is still an
      abstract concept.
   d. physicists work with time and find it difficult to explain how to
      use it wisely.

2. The author states that the task of measuring time is easier
   a. than describing how it works.
   b. when only two seasons are used to divide it.
   c. than wasting it and having to account for it.
   d. when artificial light divides the day into longer periods.

3. The article suggests that a timeframe designed by humans was the
   a. day.
   b. week.
   c. month.
   d. year.

4. The replacement of sun dials with mechanical clocks
   a. allowed the measurement of time to be more regular.
   b. was introduced by the Chinese in the 13th century.
   c. divided the measurement of time into 12 portions.
   d. decreased the variability of seasonal periods of light and dark.

5. Who invented the mechanical clock?
   a. A Greek wizard
   b. Denis Waitley
   c. Andrew Carnegie
   d. The name is unknown

6. Because time is fair to everyone
   a. we can waste it without feeling that we are cheating anyone.
   b. scientists can measure our successful use of it.
   c. each person must know the worth and value of it.
   d. we all receive the same amount of it even when we misuse it.

Threads

**O, call back yesterday,
bid time return!**

William Shakespeare

7. We destroy our chances for success when

    a. we try to save time.

    b. time is considered as money.

    c. we use our time unwisely.

    d. we plan and set priorities.

8. Andrew Carnegie followed the advice of a time management expert that resulted in

    a. a loss of a great deal of money.

    b. being more productive in his use of time.

    c. a list of things to do that were never accomplished.

    d. accomplishing nothing in his busy schedule.

9. We can be judged successful in the use of our time if

    a. we simply work hard at all the things that we need to accomplish.

    b. each day we work hard at accomplishing our most important tasks first.

    c. at the end of the day we have accomplished all that we wanted to.

    d. we start using all the hours available to us during the day.

10. One time management expert says that not using our time wisely is the same as

    a. replacing our life with too much work.

    b. reversing our hard work to play.

    c. not having enough time in our day.

    d. not making good use of our lives.

Total number of correct answers: _____ / 10

Record your reading comprehension score on the comprehension chart in Appendix C.

IT WORKS!
Learning Strategy:
Self-Evaluating

READING STRATEGY CHECKLIST

Check off the strategies you used while reading and answering the questions.

_____ I reread parts of the text I did not understand.

_____ I used the context of the reading passage to help me guess the meaning of a word I did not know.

_____ I found cognates (similar things) that helped me understand the text.

_____ I used my knowledge of English grammar to understand parts of the text.

_____ Others? Write them here: _____

_____

_____

Record your reading rate on the graph in Appendix B.

Did you reach the reading rate goal you set before reading?

Each of the comprehension statements above can be classified into one of three reading comprehension categories:

- Understanding Main Ideas,
- Understanding Direct Statements, or
- Understanding Inferences.

Review your performance on the comprehension statements and record your performance on the chart provided in Appendix B.

Did you reach your reading comprehension goal set before reading?

After checking your answers, review each one that you marked incorrectly and determine WHY you missed the question.

Reading rate and reading comprehension are very individual skills to develop. You should not compare your reading rate and comprehension with other students in your class, but you should compare your own performance each time with your previous reading performances.

POST-READING EVALUATION

LEARNING STRATEGY

Managing your Learning: Evaluate what you have learned in this chapter.

Respond in writing to the following questions, then discuss your answers with others in your class.

1. What have you learned from all the readings in this chapter on understanding time?

_____
_____
_____
_____
_____
_____
_____
_____
_____
_____

2. How has your knowledge changed as a result of these readings?

_____

_____

_____

_____

_____

_____

_____

_____

_____

3. How has your attitude changed as a result of these readings?

_____

_____

_____

_____

_____

_____

_____

_____

Threads

. . . for there is a time
for every purpose and
for every work.

Ecclesiates 3:17

4. How can you balance the productive and emotional parts of your life?

_____

_____

_____

_____

_____

_____

_____

_____

_____

_____

_____

_____

_____

_____

_____

_____

AIDS: What Is Your Response?

PRE-READING EVALUATION

Respond in writing to the following questions, then discuss your answers with others in your class. If you do not know anything about the topics to be discussed, it is okay to say that you do not know. Not knowing anything about a reading topic and recognizing that you do not, is okay.

IT WORKS!
Learning Strategy:
Relying on What
You Know

1. What do you expect to learn about AIDS?

_____

_____

_____

_____

_____

_____

2. What do you already know about AIDS?

_____

_____

_____

_____

_____

Threads

Did you know . . .
People do *not* get AIDS:
- by kissing,
- by swimming in a pool,
- by shaking hands,
- by using a toilet,
- by giving blood,
- by sharing spoons, forks, or dishes,
- from mosquitoes?

TESOL Fund for AIDS and
Health Education

3. What is your current attitude about AIDS education?

_____

_____

_____

_____

_____

_____

4. What do you already do to show that you are aware of AIDS education?

_____

_____

_____

_____

_____

_____

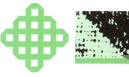

Pre-Reading Discussion

LEARNING STRATEGY

Remembering New Material: Learning common prefixes, suffixes, and stems will help you learn new vocabulary that contains these same word parts.

Knowing the meaning of prefixes, suffixes, and roots can be a strategy to guessing the meaning of unfamiliar vocabulary. Below is a list of 14 key words that use combinations of prefixes and roots. Knowing these 14 key words can lead to knowing the meanings to more than 14,000 words in English (*Nation, 1990*).

Study the list and then quiz yourself by filling in the missing information on the next page.

THE FOURTEEN WORDS

COMMON WORDS	COMMON PREFIX	MEANING	ROOT	MEANING
1. precept	pre-	before	cept	take, seize
2. detain	de-	away, down	ten, tain	hold, have
3. intermittent	inter-	between, among	mis, mit	send
4. offer	ob-	against	fer	bear, carry
5. insist	in-	into	sist	stand
6. monograph	mono-	alone, one	graph	write
7. epilogue	epi-	upon	logue	say, study of
8. aspect	ad-	to, toward	spect	see
9. uncomplicated	un-	not	plicate	fold
	com-	together, with		
10. nonextended	non-	not	tend	stretch
	ex-	out, beyond		
11. reproduction	re-	back, again	duc, duce,	lead
	pro-	forward, for	duct	
12. indisposed	in-	not	pose	put, place
	dis-	apart, not		
13. oversufficient	over-	above	ficient	make, do
	sub-	under		
14. mistranscribe	mis-	wrong	scrip, script,	write
	trans-	across, beyond	scribe	

QUIZ ON THE FOURTEEN WORDS

COMMON WORDS	COMMON PREFIX	MEANING	ROOT	MEANING
I. precept	pre-	before	cept	take, seize
2. detain	_____ 1	away, down	ten, tain	_____ 2
3. intermittent	inter-	_____ 3	mis, mit	send
4. _____ 4	ob-	against	_____ 5	bear, carry
5. insist	_____ 6	into	sist	_____ 7
6. monograph	mono	_____ 8	graph	write
7. _____ 9	epi-	upon	_____ 10	say, study of
8. aspect	_____ 11	to, toward	spect	_____ 12
9. uncomplicated	un-	_____ 13	plicate	fold
	com-	_____ 14		
10. _____ 15	non-	not	_____ 16	stretch
	ex-	out, beyond		
11. reproduction	_____ 17	back, again	duc, duce,	_____ 18
	_____ 19	forward, for	duct	
12. indisposed	in-	_____ 20	pose	put, place
	dis-	_____ 21		
13. _____ 22	over-	above	_____ 23	make, do
	sub-	under		
14. mistranscribe	_____ 24	wrong	scrip, script,	_____ 25
	_____ 26	across, beyond	scribe	

How well did you do on the prefix/root quiz? If you scored less than 20 you may want to continue studying the list and quiz yourself again. Memorizing this list will help you use this information effectively when you are reading.

Using your knowledge of prefixes and roots, with a partner guess the meanings of the following vocabulary words that will be used in the readings in this chapter.

epidemic _____

pandemic _____

solidarity _____

unprecedented _____

internationalized _____

unanimous _____

endorsement _____

collaboration _____

refrain _____

intercourse _____

uninfected _____

transfusion _____

discard _____

unwanted _____

discriminate _____

postpone _____

unprecedented _____

transmission _____

nonexistent _____

IT WORKS!
Learning Strategy:
Relying on What
You Know

Threads

You can be friends with people who have AIDS. You can go to work or school with them. You can take care of them. You can hug them.

TESOL Fund for AIDS and
Health Education

Remembering New Material: Learning acronyms helps you read smoother and faster.

Scan the article (pp. 97–98) to identify the meanings of these acronyms.

AIDS _____

GPA _____

HIV _____

UN _____

WHO _____

Set a goal for the number of words-per-minute you want to achieve before reaching the end of this passage. A recommendation is to strive to reach a minimum of 200 wpm in your reading. One factor that will be helpful in setting your goal is to review your reading rate from your weekly timed reading chart in Appendix B.

What is the reading rate goal for this passage?

Record that goal here: _____

IT WORKS!
Learning Strategy:
Setting a Goal for
Improving Reading
Rate

Reading Skill Improvement

READING RATE INSTRUCTION

Rate Buildup Reading. You will be given 60 seconds to read as much material as you can from *WHO and the Global Aids Strategy*. When your teacher says, *Stop,* write the number "1" above the word you are reading. You will begin reading again from the beginning of the text for an additional 60 seconds. Your goal is to read more material during the second 60-second period than in the first. When your teacher says, *Stop,* write the number "2" above the word you are reading. This reading rate improvement drill will be repeated a third and a fourth time. You are to write the numbers "3" and "4" above the word in the text that you reach after each 60-second period.

After the fourth minute, you will be allowed four additional minutes to complete reading the passage.

Threads

Did you know . . . one in 300 college students is estimated to be HIV positive in the USA?

Ohio University Department of Health Education and Wellness

READING 1: WHO AND THE GLOBAL AIDS STRATEGY

by World Health Organization

The World Health Organization (WHO) is the agency of the United Nations (UN) with responsibility for directing and coordinating international health work. WHO has a
5 central role in developing, coordinating, and leading the global response to the acquired immunodeficiency syndrome (AIDS) epidemic.

WHO has dealt with the epidemic in
10 three phases. The first phase, known as the "silent" phase of the HIV/AIDS epidemic, occurred in the mid 1970s to 1981. During this phase the human immunodeficiency virus (HIV) which causes AIDS spread
15 unnoticed to five continents. The second phase developed from 1981 to 1985 during which there was a period of discovery. WHO discovered more about the HIV virus, more about the modes of HIV transmission, and
20 more about the large numbers of people infected with HIV. This period was also marked by uncertainty: there were widely varying estimates concerning HIV infection rates, the precise numbers of AIDS cases and
25 the social implications of the epidemic. In many cases, individuals, communities and governments were reluctant to respond to, and even to acknowledge, the AIDS epidemic.
30 In 1985 WHO drafted a global strategy for AIDS prevention and control. This marked the beginning of the third phase of the AIDS epidemic: global mobilization. The Global AIDS Strategy was reviewed
35 and revised and, in May 1987, it was approved and adopted by the Fortieth World Health Assembly as the basis for a worldwide response to the HIV/AIDS epidemic.

40 **Three Objectives**

The Global AIDS Strategy is built on three objectives:

- prevention of HIV infection,
- reduction of the personal and social
45 impact of HIV infection,
- unifying national and international efforts against AIDS.

Preventing HIV Infection

We know that it is possible to prevent
50 the spread of HIV infection through individual behavior. Information and education about personal habits are therefore essential to the Global AIDS Strategy.

The following messages are designed to
55 give information to assist people to modify or to refrain from behaviors that carry a risk of HIV infection:

- sexual intercourse is the most common route of HIV transmission. The sexual
60 spread of HIV can be avoided by remaining with a faithful, uninfected partner or by not having sexual intercourse at all.
- HIV can be transmitted through infected
65 blood. As far as possible blood for transfusion should be tested for infection with HIV, and discarded if it is found to be contaminated. Needles and other skinpiercing instruments should
70 be sterilized after each use. An infected mother can pass HIV infection to her fetus or infant. Women infected with HIV should therefore consider avoiding pregnancy.

75 **Reducing the Impact**

The global AIDS strategy seeks to minimize the negative impact of HIV infection, both on individuals and on societies. People infected with AIDS need to
80 be given personal support and care by the people around them. They also need to be provided with health care similar to that made available in any given society to
85 people with other diseases.

Unifying Efforts

The global AIDS strategy aims to unite countries all over the world in a coordinated and effective way to prevent the spread of
90 AIDS. The worldwide effort against AIDS began with the first World AIDS Day on December 1, 1988. This showed that it is possible to unite the world in the fight against AIDS. World AIDS Day continues to
95 be an effective way to unify efforts around the world to help educate people about the spread of AIDS.

Global Program on AIDS (GPA)

WHO's GPA was established in February
100 1987 as the vehicle for putting into effect the Global AIDS Strategy. Today, GPA is working with over 150 countries around the world, helping them to develop strong national AIDS programs. It has provided
105 financial support worth over $60 million to 127 countries and technical support through more than 1,000 consultant and expert

missions for planning, training and implementing in the field. National AIDS
110 programs have been developed with great energy and much local creativity. Such programs now exist in most countries.

WHO facilitates and promotes research on HIV infections and AIDS. It designs
115 strategies for health promotion in a variety of social and cultural contexts. And it produces guidelines on a series of complex and difficult policy issues to assist local, national, and international agencies in their
120 AIDS prevention and control work.

WHO will continue to develop the Global AIDS Strategy in collaboration with national and international organizations. By continuing to collaborate with national AIDS
125 committees, provide policy guidelines and recommendations, we will contribute to the control of the global health threat of AIDS and foster the creation of a safer, healthier world for the benefit of all.

Evaluate your reading rate performance.

1. How many lines of text did you read the first minute? Write the number here: _____

2. Multiply the number of lines you read the first one-minute segment by 6. Write the product here: _____ (This is approximately the number of words that you read the first minute.)

3. How many lines of text did you read the fourth time? Write the number here: _____

4. Multiply the number of lines you read the fourth one-minute segment by 6. Write the product here: _____ (This is approximately the number of words that you read the fourth minute.)

5. What was your reading rate goal? Write your goal here: _____

6. Compare the numbers in #2 and #4 above with your goal in #5. How well did you do in accomplishing your reading rate goal?

Reading 1: Post-Reading Comprehension Check

LEARNING STRATEGY

Remembering New Material: Writing a main idea from your reading helps you remember what you have read.

Respond to the following question in writing, then discuss your response with members of your class.

How has WHO responded to the global AIDS epidemic?

_____

_____

_____

_____

_____

_____

_____

_____

READING 2: THE "AGE OF AIDS" PRESENTS A CHALLENGE TO EVERYONE

Pre-Reading Discussion

LEARNING STRATEGY

Personalizing: Talking with others before reading helps prepare you for what you will read.

Discuss the following questions in a small group, then share your response with the entire class.

1. Who is Earvin "Magic" Johnson?
2. How did Magic Johnson contract the AIDS virus?
3. What is the difference between having AIDS and being HIV positive?
4. What should you do to prevent getting AIDS?

READING 2: THE "AGE OF AIDS" PRESENTS A CHALLENGE TO EVERYONE
by Earvin "Magic" Johnson

Sexual desire is perfectly natural, and sexual fulfillment is a very important part of most people's lives. The challenge we all face is to learn how to express our sexuality in ways that respect others as well as ourselves.

5　And now, in the age of AIDS, the challenge is even greater, for we have to learn how to express our sexuality and gratify our desires in ways that don't risk the health of others or ourselves.

Sexual responsibility means more than deciding when to have sex—and here I'm talking about sexual intercourse—or with whom. It means

10　more than taking steps to avoid HIV or other sexually transmitted diseases (often called STDs) or an unwanted pregnancy. It means taking charge of your body and your choices, sorting out your feelings and values, and learning to live by them. Having sexual feelings doesn't mean you have to act on them. Some people are easily able to handle their sexual feelings

15　while others are frightened by them. Some people become sexually active earlier than others. I think the best thing you can do if you're a teenager is postpone sexual activity with another person for as long as possible. That way, you not only have a better chance of finding a lasting, loving relationship, but you won't have to worry about getting pregnant or

20　catching an STD. Some people never have sex until they're married.

Maybe you've spent time with people who are always bragging about whom they slept with. You know if you told them you were a virgin, they'd look down on you. If these are the kind of friends you've got, maybe they aren't your friends.

25　Mature people who are sexually active don't make fun of those who don't have sex. And lots of people who say they're sexually active with other people aren't. Many people feel the way you do. Go find them and hang out with them.

100

30 If you don't want to have sex with another person, you don't owe anybody a reason— it's your choice.

It's OK to have sexual thoughts and feelings. But you shouldn't feel you have to act on them until you're good and ready.

You're the one who decides when it's time to be sexually active (unless you're the survivor of rape, incest or sexual abuse), and you
35 should base that decision on your own values and beliefs. Most people rely on the values they've learned from their family, community, church or synagogue.

I'm not here to tell you that there's only one "right" reason to have sex. But before you have sex with someone, ask yourself why you want it.
40 • How do you feel about this person?
• Is he or she worthy of your intimacy and respect?
• Are you under any pressure from this person or from others to have sex?
• Are you trying to prove you're a real man or a real woman?
45 • How will having sex change your relationship with this person?
• If you never saw this person again after you had sex, how would you feel about it?

Respect the people you're with. Respect yourself the most.

How Does Having Sex Fit into Your Dreams?
50 What roles do you want sex, love and affection to play in your life? Here's one way to think about how the sex you have now can affect what you want out of life in the future:

First, think about something you're looking forward to in the future. It could be a wonderful relationship, a great place to live, a really
55 interesting career, raising a family, or all these things.

Now think about how having HIV or another STD or an unwanted pregnancy would affect your dreams. If you had HIV, you might be too sick to get what you want, or you might suffer discrimination that would keep you from fulfilling your dream, or you could die long before you
60 got your dream.

Some STDs can make you sterile so you could never have children of your own. Some STDs can make it more likely that you'll get cancer. How would you deal with an unwanted pregnancy and how would it stand in the way of your dreams? How would you feel if your baby was
65 born with HIV.

If I had known what I do now when I was younger, I would have postponed sex as long as I could and I would have tried to have it the first time with somebody that I knew I wanted to spend the rest of my life with.
70 I certainly want my children to postpone sex.

Now, the rest of my life may be a lot shorter than I thought it was going to be, and I may not be around to see my son Andre grow up and to see what happens to the baby my wife Cookie and I are having, and of course I may not have the long life I want with Cookie.
75 If you've got younger brothers and sisters, get the message to them. Tell them there'll be plenty of time for sex later. Give them the facts so that they know they're risking their lives whenever they have unprotected sex.

But just as important, tell them to really think about what they want
80 sex to mean to them, and tell them you understand what they're going through. Maybe you can reach them in ways your parents can't.

Talking to Your Partner

If you don't choose to abstain from sex, at least make a promise to yourself to talk to your partner about sex and drugs before you decide to
85 have sex with that person.

You need to know more about the person you want to have sex with than where he or she works or goes to school or lives; what kinds of music he or she likes, what other things you have in common—or even whether he or she loves you.

90 Maybe you can't picture yourself asking these kinds of questions in the heat of the moment. So don't wait until you're in bed to ask.

It takes a lot of courage to talk to your partner about sex. If you're embarrassed or worried that you might insult your partner, think about this: If you feel strongly enough about someone else to want to have sex
95 with him or her, you should be close enough to ask the questions that can protect your mutual health. How your partner responds will tell you a lot about his or her values and character.

I know this is asking a lot of you. But the silence that often surrounds sex needs to be broken if we are to have a fighting chance of eluding the
100 HIV and AIDS epidemic. The embarrassment you may feel about speaking with another about such a sensitive subject is natural.

The sad truth is that no matter what he or she says, you can never really know for sure whether someone has HIV, unless he or she has tested positive for the infection. There are several reasons for this; your
105 partner might not know he or she is infected, he or she might be in denial, or might not be being completely honest with you.

As far as other STDs are concerned, it's also true that you can never really know if a partner's been infected. A lot of people can have an STD and never know it and they can easily pass it on to anybody they have
110 unprotected sex with.

The most responsible thing to do is to act as though you and anybody you want to have sex with could have HIV and to practice safer sex every time.

So, be smart and be responsible. If you choose abstinence, you're
115 making the safest choice. You're being your own person, and wonderful opportunities for the loving, caring relationship you want still lie ahead untouched by past experience.

Reading 2: Post-Reading Comprehension Check

LEARNING STRATEGY

Personalizing: Identifying with someone in a story helps you to understand the material better because it becomes more real to you.

1. What is your reaction to Magic Johnson's advice in this reading?
2. What one piece of advice can you use in the future?

READING 3: WINNING THE WAR AGAINST AIDS

Pre-Reading Discussion

Managing your Learning: Evaluating what you have learned and how well you are doing can help you focus your learning.

Before going on with the next reading passage on AIDS, pause and reflect upon what you have learned. What new things have you learned so far? Is everything you are reading *old* material for you? What is the most important concept about AIDS that you would want to share with a friend who asks you about this deadly disease? Write your thoughts below:

_____

_____

_____

_____

_____

_____

_____

_____

Threads

Mixing alcohol or other drugs with sex impairs your judgment and reduces your ability to make wise decisions.

Ohio University Department of Health Education and Wellness.)

Reading Skill Improvement

READING RATE INSTRUCTION

Class paced reading. For this reading passage we are going to read the passage at a minimal reading rate of 180 words-per-minute. Each time the teacher calls out a number you should be near the bold-faced numbers (1 through 4.5) that you see in the margin. If you are not at the bold-faced number when the teacher calls it, skip from where you are currently reading to the number. Do everything you can to keep up with the minimal reading rate of 180 words-per-minute. If you pass a bold-faced number before the teacher calls it, keep reading. You are reading faster than 180 words-per-minute.

READING 3: WINNING THE WAR AGAINST AIDS

by DiAna DiAna

Acquired Immune Deficiency Syndrome was first diagnosed in the United States in the late 1970s. Since that time, AIDS has killed more than 204,000 Americans—half in the
5 past few years alone. Another 185,000 of the one million people infected with the HIV virus are expected to die also.

Nearly half of those diagnosed with the virus are blacks and Latinos. Women and
10 youth in rural Southern communities now constitute the fastest growing segment of people with AIDS.

Yet despite such alarming statistics, the federal and state governments have been
15 slow in implementing programs to stop the spread of AIDS. In place of government inactivity, a number of grassroots organizations have emerged.

An organization, the South Carolina
20 AIDS Education Network, was formed in 1985 to combat the growing number of AIDS cases. Like many grassroots organizations this organization suffers from a lack of funding, which forces them to make creative
25 use of the resources they have. To reach more people in the community, some of our AIDS educational programs are operated out of a beauty salon, Diana Hair Salon. **1**

The owner hands out AIDS information
30 to all her clients when they come in the shop and shows videos on AIDS prevention while they wait for their hair to dry. She also keeps books and other publications around so customers can read them while waiting
35 for their appointments.

It's amazing how many people they have educated on the job. After all, if people trust hair stylists to make them look good, why not trust them to keep us healthy as well?
40 In the past year, they have begun helping hair stylists throughout the Southeast set up similar programs in their

shops. These same people can also be valuable resources in spreading information
45 to their schools, community groups, and churches.

The organization has developed several techniques that they think may be of use to other grassroots groups doing similar work.
50 While they realize that there is no one way of winning the war against AIDS, they would like to share a few lessons they have learned in the battle against AIDS:

Speak to your community in a way they **2**
55 can hear. Many communities have a low literacy rate, making it impossible to simply pass out AIDS literature and instruct people to read it. To solve this problem, ask people in the community who can draw well to
60 create low-literacy AIDS education publications.

These books use simple, hand-drawn pictures of "sad faces" and "happy faces" to illustrate ways people can prevent AIDS.
65 They are also careful to show people who look like the ones we are trying to educate, since people can relate more when they see familiar faces and language they can understand. As a result, they have found
70 that the books actually have more effect in the communities where they work than government publications which cost thousands of dollars more to produce.

Train teenagers to educate their peers.
75 Because AIDS is spreading fastest among teenagers in the rural South, these hair stylists have established an "AIDS Busters" program which teaches youth from eight to 26 to go out into the community and teach
80 "AIDS 101" to their peers. They can break it **3** down and explain the risk of AIDS infection to friends their own age much better than an adult can. They also play a vital role in helping parents understand the types of

peer pressure their children experience.

Redefine "at risk" to include women from different backgrounds and marital status. One woman was told by her doctor that she was not at risk for AIDS because she was married and didn't use drugs. This kind of misinformation plagues the medical establishment. According to the Centers for Disease Control, women will soon make up 80 percent of those diagnosed with the AIDS virus.

In their training, these ladies emphasize that everyone is at risk. They also emphasize that everyone has a right to protect themselves—regardless of marital status.

Churches are a good resource to utilize. In the face of the growing epidemic, churches are starting to take a proactive role in educating their congregations about AIDS.

These lessons learned from fighting AIDS are by no means the only solutions to the crisis. But until there is a cure for AIDS, education represents the only safe measure **4** to guard against the virus.

Like no other plague before, the AIDS epidemic threatens to wipe out an entire generation and leave another orphaned. We must not let cultural, racial, or social barriers distract us from the job that must be done. Nor can we let political ineptitude stop us from our task. This is an undeclared war that everyone must enlist in for us to win. We simply cannot let people continue to die because we don't feel comfortable talking about AIDS. Everyone must become an educator and learn to live. **4.5**

Reading 3: Post-Reading Comprehension Check

Compare the advice given in this reading passage for preventing the spread
of AIDS and the HIV virus with advice given in the two previous passages.
What advice is the same in all? What advice is different? Make a list below:

Advice that is the same:

_____

_____

_____

_____

_____

_____

_____

_____

_____

Advice that is different:

_____

_____

_____

_____

_____

_____

_____

_____

_____

_____

LEARNING STRATEGY

**Managing your Learning: Comparing what you have
written with a partner provides a way for you to check
your comprehension.**

Compare what you have written with a partner in the class. Is your
information the same as your partner's? What is different?

Pre-Reading Discussion

Before reading the next passage on AIDS, review the following chart that contains information about the number of reported AIDS cases in the world.

AIDS Cases Reported, by Continent
(As of January 1, 1989)

CONTINENT	CASES	COUNTRIES REPORTING	COUNTRIES REPORTING ONE OR MORE CASES
AFRICA	20,905	51	46
AMERICAS	93,723*	44	42
ASIA	285	38	22
EUROPE	16,883	30	28
OCEANIA	1,180	14	5
TOTAL	132,976	177	143

*Approximately 85 percent of these cases (80,538) are in the United States alone.

World Health Organization, Global Program on AIDS

Write a response to the following questions then share your answers with your classmates.

1. What do you learn from this information?

   _____

   _____

   _____

   _____

2. Where are the greatest number of AIDS cases? _____

3. Where are the least number of AIDS cases? _____

GOAL SETTING

Set a goal for the number of words-per-minute you want to reach while reading *The World's Struggle Against AIDS.*

Record that goal here: _____

What is the reading comprehension goal?

Record that goal here: _____

READING 4: THE WORLD'S STRUGGLE AGAINST AIDS

by Cynthia G. Wagner

The mobilization of the world in response to the AIDS epidemic has been without precedent. At a time when the number of AIDS cases around the world is dramatically
5 increasing, nations are showing great solidarity in battling this common enemy—one that attacks rich and poor countries alike.

By the end of 1988, virtually every
10 nation in the world had established a program to educate its people about AIDS, according to Jonathan Mann, director of the World Health Organization's (WHO) Global Program on AIDS. At that time, 143
15 countries had reported one or more AIDS cases.

In addition to national programs designed to fight the AIDS virus, international cooperation has also
20 emerged. Through open exchanges of scientific data as well as through the support of international organizations such as the World Health Organization the nations of the world can combine efforts in
25 the fight against this deadly disease. According to WHO, this internationalized effort has produced two critical developments: First, there is an amazing level of global solidarity, with worldwide
30 involvement of scientists and international sharing of human and financial resources to fight AIDS. Second, the work of governments, organizations, and institutions has now been followed by an
35 unprecedented involvement of people—as individuals, families, and communities.

Impacts of AIDS

The emergence of acquired immune deficiency syndrome (AIDS) around the
40 globe has represented a major setback to medical progress both in the industrialized world and in less-developed countries. The past four decades saw great success in controlling infectious diseases such as
45 smallpox. Third World countries afflicted by poverty-related illnesses made great strides toward achieving "health for all by the year 2000" (a major WHO goal) through improved primary health care,
50 nutrition, sanitation, and immunization programs.

Yet, because of its sudden emergence and rapid spread, AIDS could soon wipe out this progress. By the end of 1988, more than
55 130,000 cases of AIDS were reported, but, because of under reporting, there may actually be more than 350,000 cases, according to WHO. Moreover, at least five million persons are likely infected with the
60 human immunodeficiency virus (HIV), which causes AIDS. That means as many as 400,000 new cases of AIDS could occur in just the next few years—more than doubling the current total number of cases. And
65 caring for AIDS patients could seriously strain economic resources even in the wealthier countries.

Worldwide, other diseases still claim far more victims annually than does AIDS. Each
70 year, three million people die from tuberculosis, and five million children die from dehydration due to chronic diarrhea. But AIDS has the potential to surpass other killers in the future.

75 Preventing one case of AIDS means preventing many future cases, while preventing a case of measles or malaria in Africa would have little effect on transmission, since those diseases are
80 already so widespread in many countries. And resources devoted to AIDS testing, treatment, and education could also be used to battle these other, more-pervasive diseases in developing countries.

Stopping the Spread

Stopping AIDS does not necessarily have to wait for a "technical fix" or medical breakthrough. The development of a vaccine to prevent AIDS is still some years away, according to Mann, but the spread of AIDS can be slowed even without a vaccine.

AIDS spreads only in limited ways, which can be prevented through informed and responsible behavior, says WHO.

Encouraging this informed and responsible behavior will depend on understanding the differences in the ways AIDS is transmitted around the world. AIDS is spread in three basic ways: first, through sexual intercourse; second, through exposure to infected blood; and third from infected mother to her baby. The specific patterns of transmission of the AIDS virus varies from culture to culture.

Transmission of AIDS in North America, Western Europe, Australia, New Zealand, and parts of Latin America occurs primarily among homosexual or bisexual men and intravenous (IV) drug users, largely in urban areas. Heterosexual transmission is low, but there is danger that the spread of AIDS from male IV-drug users to their female partners could increase the incidence of AIDS in the heterosexual population.

In sub-Saharan Africa and Latin America, particularly the Caribbean, most cases occur among heterosexuals, and mother-to-child transmission is common. Transmission via homosexual contact and IV-drug use is virtually nonexistent.

In Eastern Europe, northern Africa, the eastern Mediterranean, Asia, and most of the Pacific, fewer cases of AIDS have been reported thus far. Cases have generally occurred among people traveling to infected regions. While in the infected region individuals contract AIDS then return to their homes with the disease. In general, it is likely that where IV-drug use is a problem, so is AIDS—or soon will be. In Bangkok, Thailand AIDS is primarily found among IV-drug users. The World Health Organization estimates that the percentage of the city's IV-drug users infected with the AIDS virus jumped from less than 1 percent in August 1987 to 30 percent one year later.

Reaching Out

Clearly, education and prevention efforts must be targeted to meet the needs of individual countries— and even specific communities within a nation. In the United States, for instance, AIDS is spreading more rapidly among blacks and Hispanics. Homosexual and bisexual men have responded to education programs which has resulted in a dramatic reduction of new incidences of HIV infection. However, blacks and Hispanics have not responded to the education programs. A great need exists for culturally relevant AIDS information aimed at minorities. Such material could help reach these groups of potential victims of AIDS and solve the problem.

WHO believes that, as AIDS becomes more widespread, the disease has the potential to unite the world to an extent never before seen. In just two years, the global mobilization against AIDS has advanced from theory to reality, from declarations to action, they say. WHO is convinced that, together, we will dominate AIDS rather than allowing the disease and the fears, anxieties, and prejudices which surround it to dominate us.

Record your reading rate on the rate chart in Appendix B.

Managing your Learning: Evaluating your progress helps you see your improvement

Reading 4: Post-Reading Comprehension Check

Without looking back at the passage *The World's Struggle Against AIDS*, complete the following comprehension statements/questions by circling the appropriate letter.

1. Efforts to fight AIDS and educate people about the disease include
   a. countries with high numbers of AIDS cases.
   b. scientists who understand the disease.
   c. governments sharing resources to fight the disease.
   d. rich countries that can pay for AIDS research.

2. International efforts to fight AIDS include
   a. institutions working separately from governments.
   b. scientists developing a cure for the disease.
   c. the WHO taking control of the work being done.
   d. global unity and involvement of people at all levels.

3. The medical profession considers the spread of AIDS as a
   a. problem that can be solved in the near future.
   b. major setback in the progress towards decreasing the spread of the disease.
   c. minor problem compared to the spread of smallpox.
   d. disease that will spread more in Third World countries.

4. According to the text, AIDS has the potential of
   a. killing more people than any other disease.
   b. infecting people with limited financial resources.
   c. causing underreporting of cases.
   d. uniting all health providers in efforts to find a cure.

5. Today, what other diseases kill more people than AIDS?
   a. HIV infected individuals.
   b. AIDS has already killed more people than other diseases.
   c. Intraveneous drugs and tobacco products.
   d. Tuberculosis and dehydration from diarrhea.

6. More lives will be saved through AIDS prevention

   a. when there are more economic resources.

   b. than through the prevention of other diseases.

   c. in rich countries than in developing nations.

   d. for HIV-positive individuals.

7. One way that AIDS is spread is through

   a. exposure to infected blood.

   b. kissing an infected person.

   c. touching someone with the disease.

   d. breathing the air near an infected person.

8. The transmission of AIDS in Western Europe occurs in

   a. the heterosexual population.

   b. mother-to-child transmission.

   c. homosexual men, bisexual men, and IV-drug users.

   d. homosexual and heterosexual populations.

9. The spread of AIDS in heterosexuals is influenced by

   a. homosexuals' spreading the disease in large cities.

   b. male intravenous drugs users infecting their female partners.

   c. the spread of the disease from culture to culture.

   d. irresponsible behavior of AIDS-infected individuals.

10. An effective way to reduce future cases of AIDS is through

   a. scientific research.

   b. decreasing the fears of communities.

   c. action on the part of individuals.

   d. preparation of education materials.

Total number of correct answers: _____ / 10

Record your reading comprehension score on the comprehension chart in Appendix C.

LEARNING STRATEGY

Forming Concepts: Reading graphs helps you visualize reading material.

Record your reading rate on the graph in Appendix B. How does your reading rate on this passage compare with your rate on the other passages? Slower? Faster? The same?

Did you reach the reading rate goal you set before reading?

Each of the comprehension questions on page 110 can be classified into one of three reading comprehension categories:

- Understanding Main Ideas,
- Understanding Direct Statements, or
- Understanding Inferences.

Review your performance on each question and record your performance on the chart provided in Appendix C. How does your reading comprehension on this passage compare with the previous passages? Lower? Higher? The same?

Did you reach the reading comprehension goal you set before reading?

After checking your answers, review each one that you marked incorrectly and determine WHY you missed the question.

Graphs create visuals that have meaning. Review you reading rate graph and reading comprehension graph in Appendices B and C.

Answer the following questions based on these graphs.

1. What do you learn about your reading rate as you "read" these graphs?

   _____

   _____

   _____

   _____

2. Is the reading rate graph consistent from chapter to chapter or is there a difference among chapters?

   _____

3. In which chapter did you have your highest reading rate?

   _____

4. Why do you think you had your fastest reading rate in this chapter?

   _____

   _____

   _____

   _____

5. In which chapter did you have your lowest reading rate?

   _____

6. Why do you think you had your slowest reading rate in this chapter?

_____

_____

_____

_____

7. What do you learn about your reading comprehension as you "read" these graphs?

_____

_____

_____

_____

8. Is the reading comprehension graph consistent from chapter to chapter or is there a difference among chapters?

_____

9. In which chapter did you have your highest reading comprehension score?

_____

10. Why do you think you had your highest reading comprehension score in this chapter?

_____

_____

_____

_____

11. In which chapter did you have your lowest reading comprehension score?

_____

12. Why do you think you had your lowest reading comprehension score in this chapter?

_____

_____

_____

_____

Threads

Did you know . . . one out of five AIDS cases in the USA occur in individuals between the ages of 20-29?

Ohio University Department of Health Education and Wellness

LEARNING STRATEGY

Managing Your Learning: Self-evaluating helps you improve your strategy use.

13. Write a summary of what you learn about your own reading based on these graphs. Then share what you have learned with a partner.

_____

_____

_____

_____

_____

_____

_____

_____

_____

_____

_____

_____

*IT WORKS!
Learning Strategy:
Evaluating Your
Reading
Performance*

WHAT HAVE YOU LEARNED?

Think about the questionnaires you completed in Chapter 1. What have you learned about your learning style and learning strategies? Has your knowledge of your learning style helped you while reading? Has knowledge of your reading strategy profile helped you while reading? Record your ideas and thoughts below.

_____

_____

_____

_____

_____

_____

_____

_____

_____

_____

_____

Discuss with a partner what you have learned about yourself.

POST-READING EVALUATION

Respond in writing to the following questions, then discuss your answers with others in your class.

1. What have you learned from all the readings in this chapter on AIDS?

_____

_____

_____

_____

_____

_____

_____

IT WORKS!
Learning Strategy:
Evaluating What
You Have Learned

2. How has your knowledge changed as a result of these readings?

_____

_____

_____

_____

_____

_____

_____

_____

3. How has your attitude changed as a result of these readings?

_____

_____

_____

_____

_____

_____

_____

4. What can you do to show that you are more aware of AIDS?

_____

_____

_____

_____

_____

_____

Threads

For more information about AIDS, or to locate the groups in your area working on education, contact:

National AIDS Information Clearinghouse, P.O. Box 6003, Rockville, MD 20849, (800) 458-5231;

Centers for Disease Control, Center for Infectious Disease AIDS Program, Atlanta, GA 30333, (404) 329-3651;

National AIDS Hotline, P.O. Box 13827, Research Triangle Park, NC 27709, (800) 342-AIDS (English), (800) 344-SIDA (Spanish)

Medical Care: Do You Have a Choice?

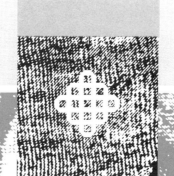

Complete the following statement by checking the goals you want to achieve in this chapter.

While working on this chapter, I will make an effort to:

_____ **1.** increase my reading rate.

_____ **2.** increase my comprehension of main ideas.

_____ **3.** increase my comprehension of direct statements.

_____ **4.** increase my comprehension of inferences.

_____ **5.** improve my vocabulary.

_____ **6.** learn more about the information in this chapter.

_____ **7.** be more aware of my reading strategies.

_____ **8.** ask more questions when I don't understand what I read.

Vocabulary Development

Many nouns in English have a verb form that is similar. Look at the following examples.

Noun Form	Verb Form
examination	to examine
practitioner	to practice
maintenance	to maintain

Below you are given the noun form of a word. Write the verb form.

Noun Form	Verb Form
1. radiation	_____
2. establishment	_____
3. creation	_____
4. interaction	_____
5. growth	_____
6. manipulation	_____
7. treatment	_____
8. demonstration	_____
9. offer	_____
10. diagnosis	_____

Below you are given the verb form of a word. Write the noun form.

Noun Form	Verb Form
1. _____	to integrate
2. _____	to perform
3. _____	to prescribe
4. _____	to survey
5. _____	to add
6. _____	to evolve
7. _____	to perform
8. _____	to practice
9. _____	to work
10. _____	to demonstrate

LEARNING STRATEGY

Learning with Others: Working with a partner to compare vocabulary helps you improve.

Compare your lists with those of a partner. Are your lists the same?

Do you see any patterns of suffixes that make a word a noun or a verb? List any patterns you see. Share your list with a partner.

_____

_____

_____

_____

_____

READING 1: ALTERNATIVE MEDICINE

Pre-Reading Discussion

SKIMMING TO DETERMINE PURPOSE

Take 60 seconds to skim the passage *Alternative Medicine* to determine what the purpose of this text is. Write one sentence which gives the purpose of this text.

*IT WORKS!
Learning Strategy:
Getting the Idea
Quickly*

_____

_____

READING 1: ALTERNATIVE MEDICINE

Adapted from Charles S. Clark

In 1994, Maureen Jensen learned she was one of the million who are diagnosed each year with cancer. The retired dentist underwent conventional surgery to have the cancer removed and followed up with a series of radiation treatments. But later blood tests showed that the cancer was still in her body. So Anderson joined the growing number of people who are turning to alternative medicine. Today, she credits her return to good health to her treatments developed by a Quebec doctor named Gaston Naessens. Alternative medicine is distinct from the accepted thinking of "allopathic" medicine, the term alternative practitioners use for conventional medicine. More and more people are turning to alternative forms of medicine not easily accepted by allopathic physicians.

Alternative medicine refers to the techniques for treating and preventing disease that are regarded by modern Western medicine as scientifically unproven to unorthodox. The term alternative medicine can encompass a wide range of therapies, including chiropractic, homeopathy, acupuncture, herbal medicine, meditation, biofeedback, massage therapy, and various "new age" therapies such as guided imagery and naturopathy. Although many alternative therapies have long been widely employed in the treatment of disease, the scientifically oriented modern medical establishment has typically been skeptical about, and sometimes opposed to, their use. In 1993 the U.S. National Institutes of Health established the Office of Alternative Medicine to examine the merits of such techniques.

If there is a unifying theme to the alternative medicine movement, it comes under the label "holistic," a school of medical thought that seeks to treat the whole person, on the assumption that we are more than just the sum of our body parts. As described by the American Holistic Medicine Association, holistic healers go beyond the "treatment only" perspective to create a system of interaction and growth that emphasizes personal responsibility and integration of body, mind, emotions and spirit.

On a practical level, that means establishing a partnership between healer and patient (or "client," as some prefer) that permits a long-term examination of the quality of the person's life. "I'm talking about fatigue, chronic pain, backaches, digestive upsets, bronchitis and a general sense of not being well," says James S. Gordon, a psychiatrist and professor at Georgetown University School of Medicine and author of several books on holistic medicine.

The therapies offered for such chronic but not life threatening ailments can include everything from massage to fruit diets to the application of electrical devices to measure the body's "energy force." A patient's interest in one unconventional treatment frequently leads to another, as information is spread through word of mouth at such places as health food stores.

Inquirers find themselves drawn into ancient Eastern views of the relationship between mind and body. The notion of the energy field in the body doesn't correspond with Western thinking.

Will alternative medicine replace traditional medicine? It is not likely, but many people today are at least considering alternative medicine as an additional source of help when illness occurs.

LEARNING STRATEGY

Forming Concepts: Summarizing the main idea after you skim a text helps you remember what you have read.

What is the main idea of the passage *Alternative Medicine*?

_____

_____

_____

_____

_____

_____

_____

Share what you have written with a partner. Do you have ideas that are the same? If your statement of the main purpose of *Alternative Medicine* is not the same as your partner's, how is it different?

Read *Alternative Medicine* again carefully. As you read the passage, see if your statement of the main purpose is accurate.

IT WORKS!
Learning Strategy:
Cooperating with
Peers

Reading 1: Post-Reading Comprehension Check

Answer the following questions:

1. List four therapies that are part of alternative medicine.

   a. _____

   b. _____

   c. _____

   d. _____

2. How does the article define the term "holistic"?

   _____

   _____

   _____

   _____

3. According to alternative medicine practices, the patient is considered part of the healing process. True or False. Why?

_____

_____

_____

_____

_____

4. Does the author think that alternative medicine will replace traditional medicine? Why?

_____

_____

_____

_____

_____

5. Was your written statement of the main idea (completed in the pre-reading section) correct? If it was not, how would you change your statement of the main purpose now that you have carefully read the article?

_____

_____

_____

_____

_____

LEARNING STRATEGY

Remembering New Material: Sharing your ideas after reading helps you to remember better and longer.

Share your responses to the questions above with a small group. Do you all agree on your answers? Why don't you agree? Check the text to justify your answers and explain your justification to your group members.

Pre-Reading Discussion

What is your opinion? Can alternative medicine and conventional medicine exist together?

_____

_____

_____

_____

_____

_____

_____

_____

_____

_____

LEARNING STRATEGY

Forming Concepts: Forming your own opinion helps you understand what you read.

Read *Two Perspectives on Alternative Medicine*. If you agree that alternative medicine and conventional medicine can exist together, read the *YES!* perspective first. If you think that they cannot exist together, read the *NO!* perspective first. After you read the passage that supports your opinion, read the other passage.

READING 2: TWO PERSPECTIVES ON ALTERNATIVE MEDICINE

**CAN ALTERNATIVE MEDICINE COEXIST
WITH CONVENTIONAL MEDICINE?**

YES!

by Dr. C. Norman Shealy and Caroline M. Myss

Traditional and holistic practitioners have much to learn from one another. The holistic world is not a fad; it marks a major turning point in the evolution of our understanding. Indeed, this unified concept is much more scientific, even though we do not yet have all the facts to
5 support the interrelationships. Bringing in intuitive influence leads one to accept that there is a capacity to influence consciousness.

In fact, once science acknowledges adequately the crucial nature of intuition as the basis for discovery, it will become possible to include, in medical school, courses in development of intuitive skills. Physicians
10 will benefit from the expansion of personal ability, and the quality of medical practice will take a leap forward.

As we move toward a medical standard for the 21st century, physicians and other health care professionals will work as teams. The days of practitioners working alone are passing. No one person can
15 integrate all the facts. Patients will be recognized as part of the healing team.

Manipulation of the spine will be an integral part of evolution and treatment, as well as massage. Acupuncture and various forms of electrical and electromagnetic therapy will be coupled with the use of
20 music and sound to assist in balancing the human system. Nutrition and a healthy lifestyle will be taught and exemplified by all the team members. Relaxation techniques will be essential components, as will a comprehensive exercise program, including aerobic exercise and yoga. The concepts of natural medicine will become a standard part of
25 medicine.

Spiritual healing will provide the framework for all the related physical, chemical and behavioral approaches. Therapeutic touch and other forms of "laying on of hands" will be as accepted as aspirin. Drugs and surgery will remain as secondary alternatives, to be used as giant
30 Band-Aids in serious situations, to hold patients over until they can develop the strength to enter consciously the path to their own spiritual transformation, to express fully the light of the Soul.

Shealy is a neurosurgeon and the founder of the
American Holistic Medical Association;

Myss is a "human consciousness lecturer."

NO!

by Dr. Stephen Barrett

During the past year, the news media have publicized "alternative" methods in ways that will cause public confusion. Most of these reports have contained little critical thinking and have featured the views of proponents and their satisfied clients. And many have suggested that
5 "alternative" methods have become increasingly accepted by the public, even though no valid data exist to compare past and present utilization.

In January 1993, The New England Journal of Medicine published "Unconventional Medicine in the United States." The article was based on a telephone survey of 1,539 individuals concerning the use of 16
10 types of "unconventional therapy." The authors conclude: "In 1990 Americans made a estimated 425 million visits to providers of unconventional therapy. This number exceeds the number of visits to all United Stated primary-care physicians (388 million). Expenditures . . . amounted to approximately $13.7 billion."

15 This conclusion is misleading. The authors define "unconventional therapies" as "medical intervention not taught widely at U.S. medical schools or generally available at U.S. hospitals." However, the categories they selected include some approaches that are medically appropriate and some that may or may not be appropriate. Thus the estimated
20 expense total is meaningless.

"Alternative" practitioners typically use anecdotes and testimonials to promote their practices. When someone feels better after having used a product or procedure, it is natural to credit whatever was done. This can be misleading, however, because most ailments resolve themselves
25 and those that persist can have variable symptoms. Even serious conditions can have sufficient day-to-day variation to enable quack methods to gain large followings.

When challenged about the lack of scientific evidence supporting what they espouse, promoters of quackery often claim that they lack the
30 money to carry out research. However, preliminary research does not require funding or even take much effort. The principle ingredients are careful clinical observations, detailed record-keeping and long-term follow-up to "keep score." Proponents of "alternative" methods almost never do any of these things. Should scientific studies come out
35 negative, proponents invariably claim that the trials were biased and conducted improperly.

It is often suggested that if doctors were more attentive, their patients would not turn to quacks. But blaming the medical profession for quackery's success would be like blaming astronomers for the
40 popularity of astrology. The main reason for quackery's success is its ability to seduce people who are unsuspecting or desperate.

Barrett is a psychiatrist and board member
of the National Council Against Health Fraud

Reading 2: Post-Reading Comprehension Check

LEARNING STRATEGY

Forming Concepts: Defending your position helps you think through your arguments.

DEBATE

Students who share the YES! perspective meet in one group. Those who share the NO! perspective meet in another group. Each group should prepare a list of arguments supporting their position. The arguments can be taken from either of the two articles read so far or from a student's personal experience. The lists of arguments will be used in a class debate.

Each side will have ten minutes to present their arguments. The *YES!* side will present their arguments first, followed by the *NO!* side. A five minute *intermission* will then be given to allow each side to think of arguments to refute their opponents' statements. Then each side will be given five minutes to refute their opponents arguments. The *NO!* side will present first, followed by the *YES!* side.

READING 3: YOU'RE THE PATIENT—YOUR RIGHTS AND RESPONSIBILITIES

Pre-Reading Discussion

Answer the following questions with a small group of classmates.

1. Have you ever been a patient in a hospital?
2. Why were you in the hospital?
3. How long did you stay in the hospital?
4. Do you have one doctor who takes care of your health care needs?
5. Do you feel you have a good relationship with your doctor?
6. Do you keep a medical record of illnesses, vaccinations, and your general health?

Personalizing: Discussing a topic with your classmates before reading can help you understand better what you read.

While reading the passage *You're the Patient,* pay close attention to what you are thinking as you read. After reading you will be asked to verbalize your thinking to a partner and explain the reading strategies you were using.

READING 3: YOU'RE THE PATIENT—YOUR RIGHTS AND RESPONSIBILITIES

by the American Osteopathic Association

As osteopathic physicians we are especially sensitive to our patients' needs and concerned about the quality of medical care they receive. A recent nationwide health care survey we commissioned raised a number of important criticisms of the medical profession and the American 5 health care system. In response to those disturbing findings, we've put together a patient's bill of rights. As a patient, you have responsibilities to maintain your health and to work with your physician as an honest, conscientious and active participant in preserving and restoring your physical well being. And you have certain rights that enable you to be a 10 partner with your physician. The best patient is the one who is informed, aware and able to help in making and carrying out intelligent decisions about his own health.

Question: What choice do I have in choosing my physician?
Answer: You have the right to choose any physician you want to treat
15   you, and the right to stop seeing any physician with whom you're not comfortable.

Question: What should I know when choosing a physician for my family?
Answer: You have the right to be told the name of the physician
20   responsible for your care, his medical background (i.e., training and specialty) and his experience in treating problems such as yours.

Question: What kind of care do I as a patient have the right to expect?
Answer: You have the right to be treated in a humane and dignified
25   manner by your physician and by members of his staff. If you are uncomfortable with your physician's manner or attitude, you should discuss the problem with him. If he is unable or unwilling to adjust, you should find yourself another physician.

Threads

A fact about osteopathic physicians . . . by the year 2000, it is expected that 45,000 osteopathic physicians will be in practice in the United States

American Osteopathic Association

Threads

A fact about osteopathic physicians . . . over half of all D.O.s practice in the primary care areas of general practice, internal medicine, obstetrics/gynecology and pediatrics.

American Osteopathic Association

30 *Question:* In general, what kind of information can I expect my physician to give me?

Answer: You have the right to expect complete and current information about the diagnosis of your illness, the recommended and alternative forms of treatment and the
35 prognosis of your case. All this information should be given in terms you can understand. You should also be given all necessary information so that you can give your informed consent before treatment begins, such as a description of the treatment, any medical risks involved with the treatment and
40 the length of time for recovery.

Question: Can I refuse treatment that I don't want?

Answer: It is your right to refuse treatment if you choose. If you do refuse treatment, your physician has the responsibility to inform you of the medical consequences of your decision.

45 *Question:* What about the confidentiality of my illness and treatment?

Answer: Physicians have a legal obligation to protect your privacy in medical matters. Anyone not directly involved in your treatment must obtain your permission before becoming involved in the discussion of your case or in conducting your
50 examination or treatment. You also have the right to expect your physician's staff to treat your medical records as confidential.

Question: What right do I have to my medical records?

Answer: You have the right to information contained in your personal
55 medical records. Your physician should supply this information to you upon request.

Question: What if my physician isn't available when I need him?

Answer: You have the right to expect continuity of care. You should be notified of your physician's schedule and of arrangements
60 he's made for your care in his absence.

Question: What about the amount of time spent waiting to see the physician?

Answer: When you have an appointment, you have the right to expect prompt medical treatment, except when a medical
65 emergency causes an unforeseen delay.

Question: What information should I expect about the cost of treatment and payment of the bill?

Answer: At your first visit, you and your physician should have a frank discussion about the cost of the treatment, his billing
70 practices and various methods of payments available to you.

LEARNING STRATEGY

Managing Your Learning: Verbalizing your strategies helps you to be more aware of what you do as you read.

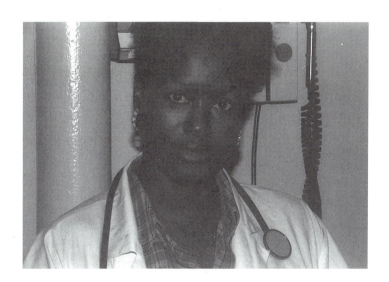

With a partner, verbalize what you were thinking while reading *You're the Patient.* Describe your reading strategies. Keep in mind that there are no right or wrong strategies to use while reading. We learn from each other as we share how we read.

READING 4: WHAT IS A D.O.?

Pre-Reading Discussion

Discuss the following questions with a partner:

1. Before reading this chapter, had you ever heard of osteopathic medicine?
2. Where had you heard the term?
3. Based on what you have read in this chapter so far, what is a Doctor of Osteopathy?
4. Do you know of any differences between a D.O. and an M.D.?

You are now going to read the passage, *What Is a D.O.?* What is the overall reading rate goal you are working towards?

Record that goal here: _____

What is your reading comprehension goal?

Record that goal here: _____

IT WORKS!
Learning Strategy:
Discussing
Questions Before
Reading

IT WORKS!
Learning Strategy:
Setting Goals and
Objectives

READING 4: WHAT IS A D.O.?

by American Osteopathic Association

The body is not a group of unrelated parts, but rather it functions as a whole. You are more than just the sum of your body parts. That is why doctors of osteopathic medicine
5 (D.O.s) practice a "whole person" approach to medicine. Instead of just treating specific symptoms, osteopathic physicians concentrate on treating you as a whole person.

10 If you are like most people, you have been going to a doctor since you were born, and perhaps were not aware whether you were seeing a D.O. (Osteopathic Physician) or an M.D. (Allopathic Physician). You may
15 not even be aware that there are these two types of complete physicians.

The fact is, both D.O.s and M.D.s are complete physicians. They are both licensed to practice medicine, perform surgery and
20 prescribe medication in all fifty states of the United States. Is there any difference between these two kinds of doctors? Yes. And no.

D.O.s and M.D.s Are Alike in Many Ways

25 • Applicants to both D.O. and M.D. colleges typically have a four-year undergraduate degree with an emphasis on science courses.
• Both D.O.s and M.D.s complete four
30 years of basic medical education.
• After medical school, both D.O.s and M.D.s can choose to practice in a specialty area of medicine—such as psychiatry, surgery or obstetrics—after
35 completing a residency program (typically two to six years of additional training).
• Both D.O.s and M.D.s must pass comparable licensing examinations.
40 • D.O.s and M.D.s both practice in fully accredited and licensed hospitals and medical centers.
• D.O.s comprise a separate, yet equal branch of medical care.

45 • Together, D.O.s and M.D.s enhance the state of care available.
However, it is the ways that D.O.s and M.D.s are different that can bring an extra dimension to healthcare.

50 ### One Hundred Years of Unique Care

Osteopathic medicine is a unique form of American medical care that was developed in 1874 by Andrew Taylor Still, M.D. Dr. Still was dissatisfied with the
55 effectiveness of 19th century medicine. He believed that many of the medications of his day were useless or even harmful. Dr. Still was one of the first in his time to study the attributes of good health so that he
60 could better understand the process of disease. Dr. Still organized the first osteopathic college at Kirksville, Missouri in 1892.

Dr. Still founded a philosophy of
65 medicine based on ideas that date back to Hippocrates, the Father of Medicine. The philosophy focuses on the unity of all body parts. He identified the musculoskeletal system as a key element of health. He
70 recognized the body's ability to heal itself and stressed preventive medicine, eating properly and keeping fit. The doctor is not a healer, but a facilitator who assists the body's natural ability to heal itself. This
75 was a new and somewhat unusual philosophy in the late 1800s when it was first presented.

Dr. Still pioneered the concept of "wellness" 100 years ago. In today's terms,
80 personal health risks—such as smoking, high blood pressure, excessive cholesterol levels, stress and other lifestyle factors—are evaluated for each individual. In coordination with appropriate medical
85 treatment, the osteopathic physician acts as a teacher to help patients take more responsibility for their own well being and change unhealthy patterns.

Sports medicine is also a natural
90 outgrowth of osteopathic practice, because
of its focus on the musculoskeletal system,
osteopathic manipulative treatment, diet,
exercise, and fitness. Many professional sports
team physicians, Olympic physicians and
95 personal sports medicine physicians are D.O.s.

Twenty-first Century, Frontier Medicine

Just as Dr. Still pioneered osteopathic
medicine on the Missouri frontier in 1874,
today osteopathic physicians serve as
100 modern day medical pioneers.

They continue the tradition of bringing
healthcare to areas of greatest need:

- While most M.D.s are specialists, most
  D.O.s are primary care doctors. Over
105 half of all osteopathic physicians
  practice in primary care areas, such as
  pediatrics, general practice
  obstetrics/gynecology and internal
  medicine.
110 - Many D.O.s fill a critical need for family
  doctors by practicing in small towns and
  rural areas.

Today osteopathic physicians continue
to be on the cutting edge of modern
115 medicine. In every state in the United States,
people who have graduated from recognized
osteopathic schools are eligible to be
licensed as physicians and surgeons. D.O.s
are able to combine today's awesome
120 medical technology with the tools of their
ears, to listen carefully to their patients; their
eyes, to see their patients as whole persons;
and their hands, to diagnose and treat injury
and illness.

125 **Some Facts About Osteopathic Physicians**

- By the year 2000, it is expected that
  45,000 osteopathic physicians will be in
  practice in the United States.
- Over half of all D.O.s practice in the
130 primary care areas of general practice,
  internal medicine, obstetrics/
  gynecology and pediatrics.
- D.O.s represent 5.5 percent of the
  total U.S. physician population
135 and 10 percent of all U.S.
  military physicians.

- Each year, 100 million patient visits are
  made to D.O.s.
- Strong concentrations of D.O.s are
140 found in Florida, Michigan, Missouri,
  New Jersey, Ohio, Pennsylvania and
  Texas.

D.O.s Bring Something Extra to Medicine

The specialized training of D.O.s adds to
145 the practice of medicine.

- Osteopathic medical schools emphasize
  training students to be primary care
  physicians.
- D.O.s practice a "whole person"
150 approach to medicine. Instead of just
  treating specific symptoms or illnesses,
  they regard your body as an integrated
  whole.
- Osteopathic physicians focus on
155 preventive healthcare.
- D.O.s receive extra training in the
  musculoskeletal system—your body's
  interconnected system of nerves,
  muscles and bones that make up two-
160 thirds of its body mass. This training
  provides osteopathic physicians with a
  better understanding of the ways that
  an injury or illness in one part of your
  body can affect another. It gives D.O.s
165 a therapeutic and diagnostic advantage
  over those who do not receive
  additional specialized training.
- Osteopathic manipulative treatment
  (OMT) is incorporated in the
170 training and practice of osteopathic
  physicians. With OMT, osteopathic
  physicians use their hands to diagnose
  injury and illness and to encourage
  your body's natural tendency toward
175 good health.

By combining all these principles, D.O.s
offer their patients the most comprehensive
care available in medicine today.

ENDING TIME: _____ : _____
TOTAL TIME: _____
1081 WORDS ÷ _____ MIN = _____ WORDS/MIN

131

Record your reading rate on the rate chart in Appendix B.

Reading 4: Post-Reading Comprehension Check

Without looking back at the passage *What Is a D.O.?*, complete the statements by circling the correct letter.

1. The primary approach of Osteopathic physicians is to

   a. practice medicine, perform surgery, and prescribe medication.

   b. specialize in areas such as internal medicine and emergency care.

   c. enhance the state of medical care available.

   d. treat the whole person not just the specific symptoms.

2. The similarities between D.O.s and M.D.s suggests that

   a. there are no significant differences between the two types of physicians.

   b. D.O.s receive as much, and perhaps more, medical training than M.D.s.

   c. M.D.s bring a new dimension to healthcare which D.O.s should also apply.

   d. both types of physicians are concerned about the concept of wellness.

3. Dr. Still introduced osteopathic medicine in reaction to

   a. Allopathic physicians' focus on the musculoskeletal system.

   b. smoking, high blood pressure, excessive cholesterol levels, and stress.

   c. the use of medication rather than the prevention of illness.

   d. the lack of adequate medical training for doctors.

4. Who is known as the "Father of Medicine"?

   a. Osteopathic physicians

   b. Dr. Andrew Still

   c. Allopathic physicians

   d. Hippocrates

5. Osteopathic physicians help to teach patients

   a. they are responsible for their own health.

   b. how to take appropriate medicines.

   c. how to be their own physician.

   d. that surgery and medicine are harmful.

Threads

A fact about osteopathic physicians . . . D.O.s represent 5.5 percent of the total U.S. physician population and 10 percent of all U.S. military physicians.

American Osteopathic Association

6. D.O.s provide basic services that

   a. allow the patient to always be in control of the care.

   b. serve people in locations which are often overlooked.

   c. M.D.s are not trained to provide.

   d. are less expensive to give complete medical care.

7. In addition to using medical technology, D.O.s use

   a. their ears, eyes, and hands to treat illness.

   b. the same resources as all M.D.s

   c. only those medicines that patients agree with.

   d. safe and careful tools to remove disease from the body.

8. D.O.s do not just treat an illness, they use

   a. large doses of drugs to make it easier for the body to heal itself.

   b. herbs and natural medicines, as well as religious healing to help the patient.

   c. the "whole person" approach, emphasizing the person rather than the disease.

   d. folk medicine and cultural traditions to help the patient understand the illness.

9. The specialized training of a D.O. gives them an advantage because

   a. M.D.s focus only on treating the injury or illness.

   b. they examine how an illness affects the whole body.

   c. over half of the D.O.s in the United States practice primary care.

   d. M.D.s focus only on high blood pressure and diet.

10. Patients receive complete medical care from D.O.s because

   a. it is not as expensive to diagnose illness through OMT.

   b. they focus on preventing illness not just curing illness.

   c. the training of a D.O. is in primary medicine.

   d. they combine many principles of medical treatment.

Total number of correct answers: _____ / 10

Record your reading comprehension score on the comprehension chart in Appendix C.

READING STRATEGY CHECKLIST

IT WORKS!
Learning Strategy:
Self-Evaluating

Check off the strategies you used while reading and answering the questions.

_____ I used my general knowledge of the topic while reading and answering the questions.

_____ I skipped words I do not know.

_____ I used my knowledge of prefixes and suffixes to guess the meaning of words I did not know.

_____ I chose my answer by eliminating choices that did not seem reasonable.

_____ Others? Write them here: _____

_____

_____

_____

_____

LEARNING STRATEGY

Managing Your Learning: Evaluating your progress helps you work toward your goal.

Record your reading rate on the graph in Appendix B.

Did you reach the reading rate goal which you set before reading?

Each of the comprehension questions above can be classified into one of three reading comprehension categories:

- Understanding Main Ideas,
- Understanding Direct Statements, or
- Understanding Inferences.

Review your performance on each question and record your performance on the chart provided in Appendix C.

Did you reach your reading comprehension goal set before reading?

After checking your answers, review each one that you marked incorrectly and determine WHY you missed the question.

Respond in writing to the following questions, then discuss your
answers with others in your class.

1. What have you learned from all the readings in this chapter on
   alternative medicine?

   _____

   _____

   _____

   _____

   _____

   _____

   _____

2. How has your knowledge changed as a result of these readings?

   _____

   _____

   _____

   _____

   _____

   _____

   _____

3. How has your attitude changed as a result of these readings?

   _____

   _____

   _____

   _____

   _____

   _____

   _____

   _____

> **Threads**
>
> **A fact about osteopathic
> physicians . . . strong
> concentrations of D.O.s
> are found in Florida,
> Michigan, Missouri,
> New Jersey, Ohio,
> Pennsylvania, and Texas.**
>
> American Osteopathic
> Association

4. What can you do to show that you have an increased knowledge of alternative medicine?

_____

_____

_____

_____

_____

_____

_____

5. Look back at the goals you set at the beginning of this chapter.
  a. Which goals did you achieve?

_____

_____

_____

_____

_____

_____

  b. What will be your primary goal in the next chapter?

_____

_____

_____

_____

_____

_____

The Information Superhighway: Are You Ready to Enter?

CHAPTER 7

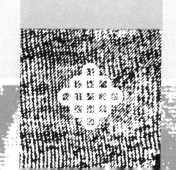

PRE-READING BRAINSTORM

What is a brainstorm? You list as many ideas as you can about a topic without taking time to judge or evaluate their importance. In a brainstorm your objective is to generate as many ideas in a limited amount of time as possible.

Your brainstorm task for this chapter is to list as many ideas and/or questions as you can about the concept of computers and the information superhighway. Your teacher will give you five minutes to brainstorm.

_____
_____
_____
_____
_____
_____
_____
_____
_____
_____

With your list of ideas and/or questions, meet with a partner and share your lists. Together generate a new list of at least five ideas or questions you would like to share with the class.

1. _____
   _____

2. _____
   _____

3. _____
   _____

4. _____
   _____

5. _____
   _____

LEARNING STRATEGY

Forming Concepts: Expanding your vocabulary helps you increase your reading rate and comprehension.

Preparing to Read: Vocabulary

Check either Yes or No to indicate if you know or do not know the vocabulary that follows.

NOTE Recall the use of Latin prefixes and roots discussed in Chapter 5.

	YES	NO		YES	NO
electronic	____	____	network	____	____
transmission	____	____	cyberspace	____	____
fiber optic cable	____	____	interactive	____	____
mega industry	____	____	technology revolution	____	____
high tech	____	____	artificial intelligence	____	____

Use the vocabulary you know in sentences. Look up the vocabulary you do not know in a dictionary, then use it in a sentence.

1. _____
   _____
2. _____
   _____
3. _____
   _____
4. _____
   _____
5. _____
   _____
6. _____
   _____
7. _____
   _____
8. _____
   _____
9. _____
   _____
10. _____
   _____

LEARNING STRATEGY

Managing Your Learning: Sharing information with partners is a good way to practice vocabulary.

Share your list above with a partner in your class.

Pre-Reading Discussion

Working in small groups, use the vocabulary above to answer the following questions. Your answers will prepare you for the readings in this chapter on the Information Superhighway.

1. Do you currently own or use a computer?
2. What do you use the computer for?
3. Have you watched the movie Star Trek or some other science fiction movie that uses computers or other high tech machines to accomplish daily tasks?
4. Where is the technology revolution taking us?
5. What should we watch for in the technology revolution?

IT WORKS!
Learning Strategy:
Setting a Goal
for Improved
Reading Rate

GOAL SETTING

What is your reading rate goal for this passage?

Record that goal here: _____

Reading Skill Improvement

READING RATE INSTRUCTION

Rate Buildup Reading. Complete four 60-second rate buildup segments. Remember to push yourself without skipping words. Read more material each 60-second period.

READING 1: A BRAVE NEW WORLD

by Tod Olson and Eric Gershon

Pick up a newspaper or turn on the TV and you're likely to think you've landed in the middle of the latest Star Trek movie. Scientists are duplicating human embryos, inventing computers that make you feel you're skiing in the Rockies, and talking about "information highways"
5 that could allow you to browse electronically through a library 6,000 miles away.

You are living through a technological revolution that is turning science fiction into reality. Where is this revolution taking us? And are there any dangers to watch out for? What follows is a look at what lies
10 ahead.

Communications and Information

Want to see Pearl Jam live . . . in Tokyo? Talk to a French teacher . . . in Paris? Tour a mall . . . in Mexico City? If all goes according to plan, you'll be able to do each of these things, without leaving your living room.

15   These are only a few of the things that you may see on the information superhighway, a blueprint for an electronic communications network that will go into every home and business. Through a single computerlike device, you would get everything from telephone service to music to videos.

20   Sounds great. But how far can we go on the infoway? And what will the view look like as we ride along it?

The Technology

Fiber Optics: The mechanism that will allow the infoway to transmit so much information is fiber-optic cable. Fiber optics are made up of 25 tiny, thin strands of glass that carry 250,000 times more information than standard copper telephone wires. That means that audio and video signals and electronic text can all be sent through a single cable.

The Home Information Appliance: This is the device you'll use to get into the infoway. It has yet to be built, but when it is, it will be a kind of 30 phone, TV, and computer, all rolled into one.

What Exists Now

The Internet: A computer network linking some 25 million people internationally, the Internet is a prototype of the infoway. On it, you can get all kinds of data—from serious scientific research to articles in 35 popular magazines—and communicate electronically with anyone who is also hooked up.

Interactive Cable TV: Some cable systems already allow users to play video games, call up magazine articles and movies, or send electronic Christmas cards—all through their TV sets.

40 **What's Coming**

Interactive Shopping: Though you may still want to go to the Gap, you will also be able to browse and order products through video catalogues.

Entertainment: You may be able to choose from as many as 500 TV 45 channels, select any movie or CD you want, or play interactive video games.

Interactive Education: Electronic card catalogues, live online classes, and opportunities to communicate easily with people in other countries are all on tap.

50 Virtual Reality: The most exciting of the new technologies, virtual reality, will allow you to simulate three-dimensional physical experiences through a computer. By putting on electronic gloves, a helmet, and other gear you will be able to interact with characters in a video game, tour a mall, or take a hike in a rain forest.

55 **Problems**

Who's paying? It is still not clear who will pay the estimated $500 billion needed to build the infoway. And once it is built, access fees may be so high that only the rich will be able to use it.

Can our privacy be protected? The more that people are connected 60 electronically, the more chance there is that someone will end up eavesdropping on you, examining your buying habits, or checking your tax records.

Threads

To err is human, but to really foul things up requires a computer.

Anonymous

142

CHAPTER 7
THE INFORMATION
SUPERHIGHWAY: ARE YOU
READY TO ENTER?

Evaluate your reading rate performance.

1. How many lines of text did you read the first time? Write the number here: _____

2. Multiply the number of lines you read the first one-minute segment by 11. Write the product here: _____ (This is approximately the number of words that you read the first minute.)

3. How many lines of text did you read the fourth time? Write the number here: _____

4. Multiply the number of lines you read the fourth one-minute segment by 11. Write the product here: _____ (This is approximately the number of words that you read the fourth minute.)

5. What was your reading rate goal? Write your goal here: _____

6. Compare the numbers in #2 and #4 above with your goal in #5. How well did you do in accomplishing your reading rate goal?

Reading 1: Post-Reading Comprehension Check

Answer the following questions.

1. Name two things that you learned about the information superhighway.

   a. _____

   b. _____

2. How is fiber-optic cable different from standard copper telephone wire?

   _____

   _____

3. Many of the plans for the information superhighway are still ideas for the future. What can you currently do on the Internet?

   _____

   _____

4. When the information superhighway is functional, what will you be able to do?

   _____

   _____

   _____

5. List one problem that the information superhighway faces.

   _____

   _____

   _____

Managing Your Learning: Working with classmates helps you develop your language skills.

Share your responses with a partner. Do you both agree on each of the answers? On which questions do your answers disagree from your partner's? Can you find information from the text to justify your response?

WRITING

What did you learn from reading *A Brave New World?* Write down three things which you learned from reading this passage. Then discuss those three things with a partner.

1. _____
2. _____
3. _____

PREPARING TO READ: CONTENT

Personalizing: Sharing information with partners is a good way to get some idea of what to expect from a reading.

READING 2: SEE.THE.FUTURE.NOW@INTERNET

Pre-Reading Discussion

Working in small groups, use what you learned from the first reading, *A Brave New World* and what you already know to answer the following questions.

1. Do you have an Internet address? Does your class instructor have an Internet address? What is that address?
2. What do Internet addresses look like?
3. Is the Internet available only in the United States?
4. If you had an Internet address, what would you use the Internet for?
5. Where would you go to get an Internet address? Find out from your school if you can get an Internet address. Practice sending an Internet message to your teacher or a member of your class.

144

CHAPTER 7
THE INFORMATION
SUPERHIGHWAY: ARE YOU
READY TO ENTER?

While reading this passage, pay close attention to what you are thinking as you read. After reading and answering the comprehension questions, you will be asked to verbalize your thinking to a partner and explain the reading strategies you were using.

READING 2: SEE.THE.FUTURE.NOW@INTERNET

by Ken Silverstein

When a dying comet crashed into the planet Jupiter on July 16, 1994, the excitement in outer space created almost as big a bang in cyberspace. Around the world, astronomers, amateur stargazers, and others interested in space logged on to their computers to trade
5 information on crash sightings, download pictures of what they saw, and write about the wonder of it all. What made this online discussion possible was the Internet, a complex worldwide web of two million computers, woven together by telephone and fiber-optic lines.

Linking 25 million people in 137 countries, and growing by a million
10 users each month, the "Net" as it's known to users, is the closet thing to a working component of the information superhighway. Created by the United States Defense Department in the 1960s as a way to electronically link scattered university researchers, the Internet has spread with remarkable speed. Today, anyone with a computer hooked
15 to a phone line (and a subscription to an Internet connection) can get onto the Net. People can tap into many databases, library catalogues, and electronic discussion groups. Enthusiasts liken their keyboard conversations to having an electronic chat with neighbors over the fence—except their neighbors can now be anywhere in the world.

20 Despite its growth, the Internet has no central authority or formal rules. Users have come up with their own informal regulations, called "netiquette," and their own way of talking to each other. Discussion-group members rarely use their real names, for example, instead favoring names tied to electronic addresses signified by the @ or "at"
25 sign. One impressive Internet address is president@white-house.gov.

Lately, however, fears have arisen that this electronic free-for-all may give rise to commercialism. Last April, for example, a Phoenix, Arizona, law firm posted an ad on the Internet, a violation of netiquette, which prohibits commercial messages except in designated areas. In response,
30 the firm was flooded with thousands of "flames"—electronic hate mail. Still, it seems only a matter of time before advertisers move in and attempt to exploit the Net for profit.

LEARNING STRATEGY

Managing Your Learning: Verbalizing your strategies helps you to be more aware of what you do as you read.

With a partner, describe the reading strategies you used while reading *see.the.future.now@Internet*.

Reading 2: Post-Reading Comprehension Check

Answer the following questions.

1. Who created the Internet? Why?

_____

_____

2. Who controls the Internet?

_____

_____

3. What is "netiquette"? How did you guess the meaning of this word?

_____

_____

4. What is the meaning of the "@" sign? How is it used in the title of this reading: see.the.future.now@Internet?

_____

_____

5. According to the author, is the Internet an appropriate place for commercialism? Why or why not? Do you agree? Why or why not?

_____

_____

Threads

Electronic aids, particularly domestic computers, will help the inner migration, the opting out of reality. Reality is no longer going to be the stuff out there, but the stuff inside your head. It's going to be commercial and nasty at the same time.

J. G. Ballard (b. 1930), British author

LEARNING STRATEGY

Managing Your Learning: Working with classmates helps you develop your language skills.

In a small group, share your responses with your classmates. Do you agree with the answers of your classmates? Why or why not? Discuss those questions that you do not agree on. Describe the strategies you used to answer the questions.

Pre-Reading Discussion

LEARNING STRATEGY

Forming Concepts: Relying on what you already know improves your reading comprehension.

Before beginning the timed reading on the Information Superhighway, think about what you have already learned in the two preceding passages. List below the major concepts you have learned (or remembered) from what you have already read.

1. _____

2. _____

3. _____

4. _____

5. _____

6. _____

7. _____

8. _____

Threads

The sad thing about artificial intelligence is that it lacks artifice and therefore intelligence.

Jean Baudrillard (b. 1929), French semiologist

IT WORKS!
Learning Strategy:
Setting a Reading
Rate Goal

Share what you have written with your classmates.

Set a goal for the number of words-per-minute you want to reach while reading *Paving the Infoway*. Record that goal here: _____

What is the reading comprehension goal? Record that goal here: _____

READING 3: PAVING THE INFOWAY

by Ken Silverstein

Are you too tired to go to the video store but you want to see a good action movie at home? Want the latest Beastie Boys CD or a new magazine or book? No problem. Just sit
5 down in front of your home computer or TV and enter what you want, when you want it, from an electronic catalogue containing thousands of titles.

Your school has no professors of
10 Japanese, a language you want to learn before visiting Tokyo during summer break. Don't worry. Just enroll in the language course offered by the school in another district—or even another state—and attend
15 by interactive video.

Welcome to the information super-highway.

While all of the infoway's potential services won't be available for years—
20 perhaps decades—dozens of communications companies are already moving ahead with plans to bring a wide array of electronic services into your home.

The world is on "the eve of a new era,"
25 says The United States Vice President Al Gore, the Clinton administration's leading high-tech advocate.

While nearly everyone has heard of the information superhighway, even experts
30 differ on exactly what the term means and what the future it promises will look like. Broadly speaking, however, the superhighway refers to the explosive merger of today's broadcasting, cable, video,
35 telephone, and computer industries into one large all-connected megaindustry.

Directing the merger are technological advances that have made it easier to store and rapidly transmit information into homes
40 and offices. Fiber-optic cable, for example— made up of hair-thin strands of glass—can transmit 250,000 times as many data as a

standard telephone wire, or the equivalent of the entire 32-volume Encyclopedia
45 Britannica every second.

The greatly increased volume and speed of data transmission that these technologies permit can be compared to the way in which a multilane interstate allows more
50 cars to move at faster speeds than a two-lane highway—hence, the superhighway metaphor.

The closest thing to an information superhighway today is the Internet, the
55 system of linked computer networks that allows up to 25 million people in 135 countries to exchange information.

But while the Internet primarily moves words, the information superhighway will
60 soon make routine the electronic transmission of sound and images as well. That means, for example, that a medical specialist in Switzerland will be able to treat patients in Kentucky after a computer
65 review of their medical records—or that teenagers in Chicago will be able to transmit video Valentines to their boyfriends or girlfriends across town.

"Sending a segment of video mail down
70 the hall or across the country will be easier than typing out a message on a keyboard," predicts technology writer John Markoff.

Vice President Gore wants the United States federal government to play the leading
75 role in shaping the superhighway. He has proposed that the government launch a high-tech development program even bigger than the one during the 1960s that succeeded in putting a man on the moon.
80 However, in an era of smaller budgets, the United States government is unlikely to come up with the money needed during the next 20 years to construct the superhighways.

147

85   That leaves private industry—computer, phone, and cable companies—in the driver's seat. And while these industries are pioneering the most exciting new technologies, some critics fear that profit-

90   minded companies will only develop services for the wealthy. "If left in the hands of private enterprise, the data highway could become little more than an electronic mall for the rich," worries Jeffrey Chester,

95   president of the Center for Media Education in Washington, D.C.

    Poor people must also have access to high technology, says communications expert David Sobel. "Such access will be

100 crucial to obtaining high-quality education and getting a good job. So many transactions and exchanges are going to be made through this medium—banking, shopping, communication, and information—that

105 those who aren't plugged in risk really falling behind," Sobel says.

    Some experts were alarmed earlier this year when they learned that four regional phone companies that are building

110 components of the superhighway were only connecting affluent suburban communities.

    The companies denied they were bypassing the poor, but conceded that the wealthy would likely be the first to benefit.

115 "We had to start building some place," says Jerry Brown, a spokesman for US West, one of the companies, "and [that] was in areas where there are customers we believe will buy the service. This is a business."

120 Advocates for the poor want the companies building the data highway to devote a portion of their profits to insuring

universal access. Proponents of universal access have already launched a number of

125 projects of their own. In Berkeley, California, the city's Community Memory Project has placed coin-operated computer terminals in public buildings and subway stations. For 25 cents per message, anyone

130 can participate in debates conducted on a variety of computer "bulletin boards." In Santa Monica, California, debate on the homeless crisis has been greatly influenced by the homeless themselves, who air their

135 views on computers available in all public libraries.

    Marc Rotenberg, director of the Electronic Privacy Information Center in Washington, D.C., says the emerging

140 superhighway offers limitless possibilities. He marvels at the recent experience of students in Alabama, who used computers to accompany and communicate with a group of scientists trekking across the

145 Canadian outback. "In the best scenario, the superhighway can help bridge cultural divides by bringing people, information, and ideas together," says Rotenberg. "That's why we have to make sure that everybody can

150 use these new technologies."

    Many challenges face us as we move closer to the reality of the information superhighway. In order for the infoway to be of value to the most people, individuals need

155 to become informed about what is possible and how being connected will be of benefit. The possibilities are endless but in order for the infoway to become a reality, some finite steps need to be taken to get the process

160 underway.

Record your reading rate on the rate chart in Appendix B.

Reading 3: Post-Reading Comprehension Check

Without looking back at the passage *Paving the Infoway*, circle the letter that best answers the question or completes the statement.

1. The author's main purpose for writing this passage is
   a. that people will be able to do all their shopping from their home.
   b. the information superhighway will not be available for many years.
   c. that the information superhighway needs to be available to everyone.
   d. The United States will play a major role in the development of the infoway.

2. When will all the services on the Information Super Highway be available?

   a. The services are available today, for those who can pay.
   b. Several years from now, possibly decades.
   c. Within a dozen years the services will be available.
   d. As soon as services are available to everyone.

3. The Information Superhighway is made up of the following companies:
   a. computer, television, broadcasting, telephone, and cable.
   b. video stores, music stores, school districts, and electronic stores.
   c. encyclopedia companies and government agencies.
   d. highway industries, glass industries, and cable industries.

4. Why does the author use the metaphor of a highway?
   a. To show that speed is the most important aspect of the information superhighway.
   b. To show that the information superhighway can handle many users and transmit data quickly.
   c. Driving on the information superhighway is like driving on a multilane highway.
   d. Many people from many different countries can be on the information superhighway.

5. How do the Internet and the Information Superhighway differ?
   a. The Internet deals with words, while the Information Superhighway will deal with words, sounds, and images.
   b. Almost anyone has access to the Internet, but access to the Information Superhighway is limited to those who can pay.
   c. The Internet is only available to people at schools while the Information Superhighway will be available to businesses.
   d. The Information Superhighway is supported by the U.S. Government while the Internet is not.

150

CHAPTER 7
THE INFORMATION
SUPERHIGHWAY: ARE YOU
READY TO ENTER?

6. To provide the proposed services of the infoway

    a. many agencies will need to work together to make the services easy to access.

    b. new cables will need to be developed to replace the current fiber-optic cables used.

    c. information from the Encyclopedia Britannica will need to be entered on the system.

    d. much money will be needed to put in the cable and link people to the services.

7. The rich and poor do not have equal access to the Information Superhighway because

    a. only people who are employed with good jobs can get an account.

    b. private businesses make the services available only to those who can pay.

    c. those with high education, and good jobs are most interested in the infoway.

    d. exchanges on the infoway are limited to banking, shopping, and communication.

8. One concern about the Information Superhighway is

    a. that it will not be available to everyone because of the high costs.

    b. regional phone companies will not install the service correctly.

    c. it will take too long to develop the system and involve everyone.

    d. the government will be left out of the development of the system.

9. Many ways are available to provide the information superhighway services to the poor, like

    a. providing free accounts to anyone who wants one.

    b. educating those who express interest in the system.

    c. requiring all companies working on the system to provide free services.

    d. providing access in all public libraries, subways, and public buildings.

10. Even though there are challenges to getting the information super-highway in place

    a. people will have fun and enjoy the service they are paying for.

    b. the closer we get, the fewer problems there will be to solve.

    c. the educational and cultural benefits will be worth it.

    d. endless tasks will be accomplished to benefit the most people.

Total number of correct answers: _____ / 10

Record your reading comprehension score on the comprehension chart in Appendix C.

READING STRATEGY CHECKLIST

Check off the strategies you used while reading and answering the questions.

_____ I created a mental picture of what I was reading.

_____ I guessed the meaning of words I did not know.

_____ I translated some vocabulary and ideas from my native language into English.

_____ I asked myself questions while I was reading to check my own comprehension.

_____ Others? Write them here: _____

_____

_____

LEARNING STRATEGY

Managing Your Learning: Evaluating your reading rate helps you improve it.

Record your reading rate on the graph in Appendix B. How does your reading rate on this passage compare with your rate on the other passages? Slower? Faster? The same?

Did you reach the reading rate goal you set before reading?

Each of the comprehension questions above can be classified into one of three reading comprehension categories:

- Understanding Main Ideas,
- Understanding Direct Statements, or
- Understanding Inferences.

Review your performance on each question and record your performance on the chart provided in Appendix C. How does your reading comprehension on this passage compare with the previous passages? Lower? Higher? The same?

Did you reach the reading comprehension goal you set before reading?

After checking your answers, review each one that you marked incorrectly and determine WHY you missed the question.

152

CHAPTER 7
THE INFORMATION
SUPERHIGHWAY: ARE YOU
READY TO ENTER?

POST-READING EVALUATION

LEARNING STRATEGY

Managing Your Learning: Evaluate what you have learned in this chapter.

Respond in writing to the following questions, then discuss your answers with others in your class.

Threads

Man is still the most extraordinary computer of all.

John F. Kennedy (1917–1963), U.S. Democratic politician, president

1. What have you learned from all the readings in this chapter on the information superhighway?

   _____

   _____

   _____

   _____

   _____

2. How has your knowledge changed as a result of these readings?

   _____

   _____

   _____

   _____

   _____

3. How has your attitude changed as a result of these readings?

   _____

   _____

   _____

   _____

   _____

4. What can you do to show that you are more aware of the information superhighway?

   _____

   _____

   _____

   _____

   _____

Entertainment: What Do You Like to Do?

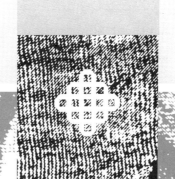

Respond in writing to the following questions, then discuss your answers with others in your class. If you do not know anything about the topics to be discussed, it is okay to say that you do not know. Not knowing anything about a reading topic and recognizing that you do not, is okay.

LEARNING STRATEGY

Forming Concepts: Relying on what you already know improves your reading comprehension.

1. In this chapter you will read about listening to jazz music in *Give Me That Jazz,* about pottery making in Ecuador in the story called *Jatun Molino,* and about game shows on TV in *The World of TV Games.* What do you expect to learn about entertainment?

   _____
   _____
   _____
   _____

2. What do you already know about jazz music? About pottery making? About TV game shows?

   _____
   _____
   _____
   _____

3. What is your current attitude about jazz music? Making pottery? TV game shows?

   _____
   _____
   _____
   _____

4. What other types of entertainment do you participate in?

   _____
   _____
   _____
   _____

Threads

Entertainment Weekly begins publication February 12, 1990. Time Warner spends $150 million to launch its first new magazine since People in 1974.

The People's Chronology

LEARNING STRATEGY

Forming Concepts: Relying on what you already know improves your reading comprehension.

Make a list of hobbies and leisure time activities you know about. Is special equipment required to participate in these hobbies or leisure time activities? Does it take special training to be good at these activities? Do you participate in any of these activities?

After you finish your list, share it with a partner.

1. _____
2. _____
3. _____
4. _____
5. _____
6. _____
7. _____
8. _____
9. _____
10. _____
11. _____
12. _____

READING 1: GIVE ME THAT JAZZ

Pre-Reading Discussion

LEARNING STRATEGY

Personalizing: Talking with others prior to reading helps you prepare to understand.

IT WORKS!
Learning Strategy:
Setting a Goal
for Improved
Reading Rate

As a class, discuss the following:

One hobby that many people have is listening to music. What kind of music do you listen to? What is your favorite kind of music? Is there one type of music that you do not like? Jazz music is becoming increasingly popular with younger audiences. Do you know any jazz artists? See what you can learn from *Give Me That Jazz*.

What is the reading rate goal for this passage?

Record that goal here: _____

Reading Skill Improvement

READING RATE INSTRUCTION

Rate Buildup Reading. Complete four 60- second reading-rate buildup segments. Try to read more during each segment.

READING 1: GIVE ME THAT JAZZ

by The Economist

Today's young jazz players just want to have fun. Back in the rocking 1960s, John Lennon summed up his generation's quarrel with jazz when he complained that "jazz never does anything": It was passive, introverted music listened to by passive, introverted people who "just sit
5   around drinking pints of beer." Rock, by contrast, was all action and involvement, a fun social exercise in which audience and musicians collaborated, releasing waves of energy and emotion. Or as one listener put it, rock was "all about sweat." In comparison, jazz was a matter of cool discrimination.
10 By the 1950s, jazz had come into its own as serious music, and jazz players demanded the same respect which classical musicians received. No one dreamed of dancing in jazz clubs. Dressed in tuxedos, the Modern Jazz Quartet was similar to a string quartet and performed with the same level of concentration. If listeners talked during the
15 performance, they might be subjected to the anger of the bandstand leader condemning their inattention. Many musicians simply ignored their listeners; in his early years, Miles Davis was known to turn his back when he played.

It was all a long way from the music's origins. In New Orleans, jazz
20 was very social, a natural accompaniment for every public occasion
from festivals to funerals. Players respected their craft but never saw
themselves as superior to their audience. As one oldtimer declared,
"When I play music I like those people around me, especially people
dancing. Then you don't think too much!"

25 As jazz developed, however—particularly with the rise of bebop after
the Second World War—a lot of musicians began thinking hard and
resenting their traditional role as entertainers. Undoubtedly the music
deserved the more serious attention it demanded, but it also gradually
left a large part of its popular audience behind, creating the vacuum that
30 rock came rushing in to fill. Rock may not have been able to match jazz's
artistic power, but it made people want to twist and shout.

Master trumpeter Wynton Marsalis recently appeared in London at a
large theater with standard concert seating—plus a large open area in
front of the stage for people to dance, stand, or walk about in as the
35 mood took them. Mr. Marsalis is usually considered to be on the high art
side of jazz, but he seemed perfectly willing to meet his audience
halfway, telling them, "You can talk if you want to; just don't scream and
holler. We're jazz musicians: We're here to swing."

But perhaps the most extreme example of jazz as an interactive music
40 took place at a recent Bath Festival. A French group known as ARFI (the
Association for Research into the Folklore of Imagination) specializes in
an amazing multimedia event that is part concert and part art show,
buffet supper, and village fete. During ARFI's three hour extravaganza,
the audience was led through a covered market by a stilt walker,
45 serenaded by jazz musicians, refreshed by wine and food prepared on
the spot, and surrounded by paper sculptures.

Jazz is the spectacle's central element. The project was initiated by a
band of musicians from Lyons who feel that action and involvement are
what jazz is all about. Whether it can also simultaneously be about
50 cooking, sculpture, and stilts may be open to doubt, but there is no
question that the relations between jazzman and jazz fan have entered a
lively new phase, recalling the music's festive origins and giving the lie
to the complaint that jazz never does anything.

Threads

The reason I'm in this business (entertainment), I assume all performers are—it's "Look at me, Ma!" It's acceptance, you know—"Look at me, Ma, look at me, Ma, look at me, Ma." And if your mother watches, you'll show off till you're exhausted; but if your mother goes, Ptshew!

Lenny Bruce (1925–66)
, U.S. satirical comedian

Evaluate your reading rate performance.

1. How many lines of text did you read the first time? Write the number here: _____

2. Multiply the number of lines you read the first one-minute segment by 11. Write the product here: _____ (This is approximately the number of words that you read the first minute.)

3. How many lines of text did you read the fourth time? Write the number here: _____

4. Multiply the number of lines you read the fourth one-minute segment by 11. Write the product here: _____ (This is approximately the number of words that you read the fourth minute.)

5. What was your reading rate goal? Write your goal here: _____

6. Compare the numbers in #2 and #4 above with your goal in #5. How well did you do in accomplishing your reading rate goal?

IT WORKS!
Learning Strategy:
Evaluating Your
Reading Rate

Reading 1: Post-Reading Comprehension Check

LEARNING STRATEGY

Forming Concepts: Making inferences helps you understand what you read.

On lines one and two, the text states: "Back in the rocking 1960s, John Lennon summed up his generation's quarrel with jazz . . . "

Who is John Lennon? Is Lennon a jazz musician? How do you know?

The text does not say that John Lennon was a rock musician with the Beetles in the 1960s. Even if you do not know this information you can infer it from the text.

Often when we make inferences we are not aware that we have "filled in missing information." The more we think about making inferences the more aware we can become of how this reading skills works.

Write down other inferences that you made while reading this passage?

_____

_____

_____

_____

LEARNING STRATEGY

Managing your Learning: Working with classmates helps you develop your language skills.

WRITING

What did you learn from reading *Give Me That Jazz?* Write down three things that you learned from reading this passage. You can look back at the text. Then discuss the three things with a partner.

1. _____

   _____

2. _____

   _____

3. _____

   _____

Pre-Reading Discussion

Discuss the following questions in a small group.

1. What do you know about making or collecting pottery?
2. Do you have any friends who collect pottery?
3. Do you know anyone who makes pottery?
4. Have you ever taken a pottery class?
5. Do you think that people who collect pottery also make pottery? Why or why not?

There is a small village in Ecuador that is famous for its pottery. Read now about Jatun Molino.

READING 2: JATUN MOLINO

by Joe Molinaro

Geographically, Ecuador is one of the most diverse countries in South America, given its relatively small size. It consists of three distinct regions; the first being the Andean range, which runs north to south throughout the interior of the country. The steep, rugged mountains rise
5 to over 20,000 feet at the snow-covered peaks of Chimborazo. To the west of these mountains are the lowlands of the coastal region that border the Pacific Ocean. To the east are the jungles of the Upper Amazon Basin, known locally as the Oriente. In the short distance of only 200 miles, one can experience the landscape from sea level to
10 snowcapped mountains, followed by a descent into steaming jungles. It is there, in the rainforest of Ecuador, that one will find the tiny, remote village called Jatun Molino.

The village has approximately 100 inhabitants (60 children and 40 adults). While the primary language is Quichua, several residents have
15 also learned Spanish as a result of traveling to the small towns that border the jungle region. There are approximately 15 houses, each strategically located along the Rio Bobanaza. Most have elevated living areas, with cooking and storage areas beneath the main floor. Palm are woven together to form the roofs; bamboo poles are split and laid for
20 the second-story flooring.

The organization of the village is communal, with all members participating in activities that contribute to the common good. The men hunt, build and repair houses, and produce baskets while the women gather foods, cook and produce pottery. Adults are the main providers
25 for the group, yet their dedication and concerns for the young are ever

present. Children are never seen as obstacles to work and are often included in jobs that might otherwise seem beyond their scope of experience. It is their involvement in the day-to-day activities that enables the Quichua to pass information on to the next generation.

30 Since most of what is learned is taught through a handed-down system, it is not surprising that both males and females readily accept their roles within the village as they grow into adults.

Even though the older women are the main producers, it is common to see young girls of 10 and 12 years old working alongside their

35 mothers and/or sisters. The older women spend time with each young potter as she carefully studies and practices the traditional production methods. While they make pottery at home for personal use, some also work collectively in a separate space that they built for the sole purpose of producing ceramic objects for sale and/or trade. These pieces are

40 transported to Quito to be sold. Selling this way is becoming more common for those inhabiting the rainforest as they seek new ways to obtain monies for medicine as well as for the tools needed for hunting and agriculture.

Whether they make their pots at home or at the workshop, they

45 conform to traditional shapes, though each nurtures personal characteristics that make the work unique. There is no "ego" behind what they make, however, and most forms and images are understood by all members of the village.

The process begins with the gathering of clay. The women hike to a

50 creek in the jungle, about a 20-minute walk from the village. They dig clay from the creek bed, filling woven palm-leaf baskets that have been lined with fresh banana leaves. Each basket holds approximately 75 pounds of wet clay. Clay is dug as needed; usually several women work together to gather enough materials for all.

55 Long hours are spent cleaning the clay by carefully squeezing it through their hands and picking out foreign particles, such as stones and twigs. Keeping the clay moist is not a problem, as the air remains humid day and night. Covering the baskets with a banana leaf is all that is required to ensure the clay will be ready for use.

60 Coiling is the main production technique. They achieve thin-walled forms by pinching added coils upward. Their tools include a variety of scrapers cut from the outer shell of dried gourds, strips of wood for paddling, small pieces of corn husks that serve as a type of chamois for the rims, and smooth stones that are collected from the river's edge for

65 burnishing. Several pieces are made at a time, which allows the potter to move on to another pot while the preceding form(s) stiffen.

When the completed pot is stiff enough, a red clay slip is applied with a cloth dragged across the surface. Once the slip has dried to the touch, fine brushes made of human hair are used to paint intricate designs.

70 These brushes are made of only one and two strands each with an overall brush length of approximately 2 inches. The pigments come from the earth (white, black, red and yellow), and are ground by hand using a large and small rock as a type of mortar and pestle. This work is extremely tedious and takes long hours to accomplish. The patterns most

75 often reflect those things that are part of daily life: animals (i.e., snakes, spiders, frogs, turtles, birds, etc.), plants and other communal imagery.

After the pots are coated with slip and the fine-line painting is complete, they are allowed to dry until ready for the fire. Forms dry

slowly in the damp air of the jungle, so potters often preheat the pieces
80 by placing them near the firing pit. Typically, pots are fired individually
in a large basin that has a 6-inch-diameter hole cut out of the bottom; it
is placed over three large logs that come together like the spokes of a
wheel. The pot is placed upside down over the hole in the basin, then
covered with wood ash, which serves as an insulator.

85   The firing requires 30-45 minutes. Once the desired time has expired,
the basin is lifted from the logs, the pot is removed and the ash dusted
off with leaves.

    The type of objects produced by the Quichua range from small bowls
called mucauas, which are used mostly for drinking chicha or serving
90 food; tinajas, storage jars of various sizes; and other large bowl forms.
They also create a variety of animal and human forms in vessel-like
configurations, all with complex surface treatment. While the forms
created by these potters has remained consistent over the years, subtle
variation and nuance are part of the quiet development of this work. In
95 addition, each artist has the freedom to explore the delicate painting as
it relates to her ability; still, the imagery remains fairly constant.

    The fragile nature of these objects is testimony to the great skill of
these potters. Their daily lives are an integral part of the work and are
reflected in the design of each piece. While others from outside the
100 rainforest may not need their ware for utilitarian purposes, many still
attach great aesthetic value to the pottery that is produced in the Upper
Amazon Basin.

Reading 2: Post-Reading Comprehension Check

LEARNING STRATEGY

**Managing Your Learning: Working with classmates helps
you develop your language skills.**

WRITING

    What did you learn from reading Jatun Molino? Write down three
things you learned from reading this passage. Then discuss those three
things with a partner.

1. _____

_____

2. _____

_____

3. _____

_____

Remembering New Material: Creating a Visual Chart from what you read helps you to remember a process described in a passage.

Lines 49–87 of the passage describe an 11-step process that the people of the village of Jatun Molino follow in making their pottery. Review these lines of the text then make a diagram that shows the process.

Compare your diagram with a partner's. Are the two diagrams exactly the same? How are they different? What changes do you want to make to your diagram?

READING 3: THE WORLD OF TV GAMES

Pre-Reading Discussion

Discuss the following questions with a partner.

1. Do you consider watching TV a hobby?
2. Is watching TV considered entertainment?
3. What kinds of TV shows do you watch?
4. What kinds of TV shows do your friends watch?
5. Are there some shows that you look forward to watching every day? every week? What are they?

Threads

**Th' only way t'
entertain some folks
is t' listen t' 'em.**

Kin Hubbard [F. Mckinney]
(1868–1930),
U.S. humorist, journalist

LEARNING STRATEGY

Personalizing: Talking with others prior to reading helps you prepare to understand.

GOAL SETTING

What is your reading rate goal? Write that goal here: _____

What is your reading comprehension goal?

Write that goal here: _____

*IT WORKS!
Learning Strategy:
Setting a Reading
Rate Goal*

READING 3: THE WORLD OF TV GAMES

adapted from Games in the Global Village *by Anne Cooper-Chen*

Television is a medium of entertainment throughout the world. After pre-war experiments in industrialized countries during the 1930s and 1940s, World War II
5 stopped the growth of television. Then in the 1950s, some 50 countries began TV services. In Japan, a commercial system to compete with the noncommercial Nippon Hoso Kyokai (NHK), was modeled on the
10 British Broadcasting System. The Soviet Union greatly expanded its state-controlled system in the early 1960s. Early adopters of television also included a number of Third World countries. Mexico, Cuba and Brazil
15 began TV operations in 1950. The Philippines followed in 1953, as did Algeria in 1956 and Egypt in 1960. By the end of the 1960s, half the world's nations had joined the TV age.
20   Because two-thirds of the world's people live in the Third World, a large number of television sets exist in Third World countries. The Third World's share of television sets increased from 5 percent in
25 1965 to 10 percent in 1975 to 14 percent in 1980 to 20 percent in 1984 to 40 percent in 1990. Part of the dramatic increase resulted from China's and India's relatively late expansion of television, in China after Mao
30 Zedong's death in 1976 and in India after the Satellite Instructional Television Experiment (SITE) broadcasts of 1975–76.
    In India, between 1984 and 1985, the number of TV viewers jumped from 37 to 60
35 million, then increased again to 90 million in 1988. During that year, television sets were sold at the rate of one every five minutes, even though a black-and-white set costs $200 to $250, or about two month's salary.
40 For those who still cannot afford this relatively high cost, the practice of community viewing increases access to

television. By the year 2000, India will have an estimated 63 million television sets, with
45 an audience of some 378 million people.
    Television is an entertainment medium, whether enough TV sets exist for almost everybody to have one all his own, as in North America, or the ratio means that a
50 roomful of people would have to share one, as in Africa.
    In 1983, entertainment accounted for these percentages of TV minutes: Asia, 48 percent; Latin America 44 percent; the Arab
55 region, 42 percent; US, 40 percent; Canada, 36 percent; Eastern Europe, 36 percent; and Western Europe, 35 percent. In only two areas, entertainment was the second rather than highest-percentage category: USSR,
60 informative content, 30 percent, and entertainment, 27 percent; Africa informative, 39 percent, and entertainment, 30 percent.
    Television is a kind, non-threatening
65 teacher for children. There is no test at the end of the show. Children watch them for the entertainment value. Moreover, TV shows can include ethnic group members, women, and children as role models. And
70 tapes can be used over and over, then erased.
    Television can be seen as a better potential teacher than live lectures, audio tapes, radio, print media, or computers
75 because television can offer voice, writing, color, still pictures, animation, and on-site depiction of events. Television can take students to places where they are unlikely to go, it can let them experience persons
80 whom they are unlikely to meet, and it can bring them inside institutions where they are unlikely to come otherwise.
    Game shows are perhaps the most popular form of television entertainment.

Game shows have endured since the beginning of television's history in many nations. Their noncontroversial, apolitical nature appeals to viewers. What makes the shows so compelling, even turning some viewers into "quiz addicts?"

A TV game show may be defined as a program featuring contestants who compete for prizes or cash by solving problems, answering questions, or performing tasks following prescribed rules. The prizes may range from large sums of cash to little more than token gifts.

The logo fills the television screen. It's the Wheel of Fortune wheel, seen by 46 million Americans on the show's daytime and syndicated versions. In France a French-language voice welcomes viewers to La Roue de la Fortune. The popular American program has not been dubbed for export; rather, only the format has been licensed.

Whether formally licensed from abroad like the top rated La Roue de la Fortune, informally adapted from abroad, or originated at home, game shows have universal appeal. Wheel of Fortune has emerged as possibly the most-watched TV show in history, with a weekly audience of about 100 million.

In Spain, four game shows regularly make the top ten rated programs. Indeed, one show, El Precio Justo (The Price Is Right) holds the all time Spanish record for advertising sales—more than $200 million in 18 months in 1990–91. In Germany, where game shows constitute the fastest-growing programming area on television, a recent hit record was titled, Life Is a Quiz Show and We're Just the Contestants.

The United States surpasses all nations in the number, variety, and subject-specificity of game shows. For example, in 1990 a viewer in the Columbus, Ohio, area could watch 34 different game shows every week. Even the nation of Belgium, with fewer than 10 million people, boasted an amazing 13 different game shows on its weekly TV schedule.

There are many reasons that media development specialists consider producing educational game shows. Game shows are: (1) Cheap because of simple sets, few paid performers, and the need for only limited creative staffing to create the skits or questions. (2) Locally produced and thus meaningful to a local or regional population. (3) Popular, judging from ratings in various countries. (4) Varied in format, such that any culture can adapt a suitable format. (5) Varied in learning, either focused or multifaceted. (6) Apolitical/Inoffensive, which gives them a run potentially long enough to have an impact and fewer problems getting funded.

Television may continue to be a primary form of entertainment for people around the world. Based on past experience, game shows will be a great part of that entertainment. It is, after all, a very inexpensive form of entertainment!

Record your reading rate on the rate chart in Appendix B.

Reading 3: Post-Reading Comprehension Check

Without looking back at the passage *The World of TV Games,* circle the letter that best answers the question or completes the statement.

1. Television viewing has increased over the years because
   a. commercial and noncommercial TV compete with each other.
   b. World War II ended and increased the number of viewers.
   c. Third World countries now allow viewing.
   d. it is a source of entertainment around the world.

2. The number of TV viewers increased in China
   a. because viewing also increased in India.
   b. after the death of Mao Zedong.
   c. because a large number of TV sets are in the Third World.
   d. when it was too late to avoid.

3. The price of a television set in India
   a. is low because of community viewing.
   b. changes every five minutes.
   c. is a worker's salary for two months.
   d. allows many people to buy one.

4. TV provides entertainment
   a. for about 50 percent of the world's population.
   b. because everyone has a TV set.
   c. in only two regions of the world.
   d. because there is very little to do in some places.

5. Television is a good teaching tool because
   a. children do not threaten the teacher.
   b. it provides role models of different ethnic groups.
   c. it tests children after they view a program.
   d. programs are shown over and over.

6. Lectures are not as educational as television programs because
   a. TV provides a visual experience that is not easy to give through words.
   b. lectures are lacking variety in presentation format.
   c. students do not have access to radio and print materials.
   d. lectures limit the focus on places and people that students already know.

7. A game show is defined as

 a. The Wheel of Fortune and The Price is Right.

 b. contestants answering questions for prizes.

 c. an American TV program exported to other countries.

 d. a set of rules for winning prizes.

8. American TV game shows

 a. do not appeal to international audiences.

 b. are limited in number, variety, and subject.

 c. are more popular overseas than at home.

 d. have been adapted in many countries of the world.

9. Media development specialists produce game shows because

 a. they cannot get funding for other productions.

 b. they do not have to make any changes to the format.

 c. they are cheap, easy to produce, and popular.

 d. they are controversial and often do not have an impact on viewers.

10. Game shows provide TV viewers with

 a. a bargain for entertainment.

 b. American shows for education.

 c. greater contact with past experiences.

 d. entertainment from around the world.

Total number of correct answers: _____ / 10
Record your result on the chart in Appendix C.

READING STRATEGY CHECKLIST

Check off the strategies you used while reading and answering the questions.

_____ I reread parts of the text I did not understand.

_____ I used the context of the reading passage to help me guess the meaning of a word I did not know.

_____ I found cognates which helped me understand the text.

_____ I used my knowledge of English grammar to understand parts of the text.

_____ Others? Write them here: _____

_____

_____

IT WORKS!
Learning Strategy:
Self-Evaluating

Managing Your Learning: Evaluating your reading rate helps you improve it.

Record your reading rate and comprehension score on the reading graphs in Appendix B. How does your reading rate on this passage compare with your rate on the earlier passages? Slower? Faster? The same?

Did you reach the reading rate goal you set before reading?

Each of the comprehension questions above can be classified into one of three reading comprehension categories:

- Understanding Main Ideas,
- Understanding Direct Statements, or
- Understanding Inferences.

Review your performance on each question and record your performance on the chart provided in Appendix C. How does your reading comprehension on this passage compare with the previous passages? Lower? Higher? The same?

Did you reach the reading comprehension goal you set before reading?

After checking your answers, review each one that you marked incorrectly and determine WHY you missed the question.

POST-READING EVALUATION

Managing Your Learning: Evaluate what you have learned in this chapter.

Respond in writing to the following questions, then discuss your answers with others in your class.

1. What have you learned from all the readings in this chapter on entertainment?

_____

_____

_____

_____

_____

2. How has your knowledge changed as a result of these readings?

_____

_____

_____

_____

_____

3. How has your attitude changed as a result of these readings?

_____

_____

_____

_____

_____

4. What can you do to show that you are more aware of different types of entertainment?

_____

_____

_____

_____

_____

Environmental Awareness: Can You Make a Difference?

9

SETTING GOALS

Complete the following statement by checking the goals you want to achieve in this chapter.

While working on this chapter, I will make an effort to:

_____ **1.** increase my reading rate.

_____ **2.** increase my comprehension of main ideas.

_____ **3.** increase my comprehension of direct statements.

_____ **4.** increase my comprehension of inferences.

_____ **5.** improve my vocabulary.

_____ **6.** learn more about the information in this chapter.

_____ **7.** be more aware of my reading strategies.

_____ **8.** ask more questions when I don't understand what I read.

READING 1: ONE STEP AT A TIME

Pre-Reading Discussion

LEARNING STRATEGY

Remembering New Material: Putting new words into meaningful sentences helps you remember them.

WORDSEARCH

Hidden in the grid on the next page are vocabulary words from the upcoming reading selections on Environmental Awareness. The words can occur forward, backwards, horizontally, vertically, or diagonally. A list of all the hidden words in the word search are listed above the grid. After you find each word, circle it and cross it off the list. One word has already been completed for you.

contaminate
damage
deforestation
depletion
ecological

endangered
environmental
erosion
extinction
global warming

hazardous
ozone
pollution
recover
waste

Word Search

C	O	N	T	A	M	I	N	A	T	E	V	H	O	T
M	K	L	G	T	D	P	O	L	U	T	F	S	Z	P
W	H	K	Y	U	E	X	T	I	N	C	T	I	O	N
T	A	R	N	K	F	P	W	Q	E	G	A	M	A	D
Z	Z	E	N	N	O	I	T	U	L	L	O	P	K	E
D	A	V	R	L	R	B	L	K	J	H	I	O	I	P
E	R	O	V	O	E	C	O	L	O	G	I	C	A	L
R	D	C	L	O	S	Y	I	N	Z	I	P	X	Q	E
E	O	E	B	W	T	I	O	N	O	P	L	M	B	T
G	U	R	M	L	A	G	O	H	N	O	P	O	Z	I
N	S	O	Z	O	T	S	L	N	E	P	V	R	C	O
A	B	L	O	P	I	T	T	I	H	Y	P	D	S	N
D	M	O	P	B	O	U	I	E	I	K	G	H	F	P
N	O	R	T	L	N	U	I	L	P	T	O	K	M	L
E	N	V	I	R	O	N	M	E	N	T	A	L	P	I
E	N	G	N	I	M	R	A	W	L	A	B	O	L	G

APPLYING THE STRATEGY: COOPERATING WITH PEERS

Working with a small group of students in your class, see if you know the meanings of the words from the word search. Make a list of the words that you know and write a brief definition on the line provided. Then use each in a meaningful sentence.

1. _____
   _____

2. _____
   _____

3. _____
   _____

4. _____
   _____

5. _____
   _____

6. _____
   _____

7. _____
   _____

8. _____
   _____

IT WORKS!
Learning Strategy:
Relying on What
You Know

Think about what you already know about environmental problems. Make a list of environmental problems you know about. Try to incorporate as much of the vocabulary from the word search as you can.

_____
_____
_____
_____
_____
_____
_____
_____
_____
_____

Reading Skill Improvement

READING RATE INSTRUCTION

Repeated Reading. The following article, *One Step at a Time,* looks at environmental problems in six areas of the world: Canada, Costa Rica, Brazil, Eastern Europe, Ghana, and Indonesia. Each section contains an environmental problem as well as the steps that the government or governments in the region have taken to solve the environmental problem.

You will read and reread each section a few times before writing the environmental problem and solution. The goal for reading is to increase your speed by reading and rereading until you have reached the goal. Your teacher will keep time for you and tell you when to begin reading each section and when to stop reading.

READING 1: ONE STEP AT A TIME

by Miles Gordon

Reading Rate Goal: 150 wpm

Directions: Read the Introduction three times in 1:15 (one minute and fifteen seconds). If you do, you will be reading approximately 150 wpm.

Reading Comprehension Goal: What is the purpose of this article?

Introduction

In most parts of the world, environmental awareness does not exist. The great majority of nations concern themselves with economic development, regardless of its effect on the global ecology. But in recent years, as environmental damage has worsened, signs of change have sprung up in various pockets around the world. The following offers a few examples of countries undertaking new environmental initiatives.

SELF-EVALUATION

Were you able to read this section three times in 1:15?   YES   NO

Continue reading the next section: Canada

Reading Rate Goal: 165 wpm

Directions: Read the section on Canada three times in 2:15.

Reading Comprehension Goal: What is the environmental problem in Canada? What steps has the Canadian government taken to solve the problem? After reading this section, write your answer to these two questions then share your responses with a partner.

Canada

When European explorers first came to the New World, the fishing grounds off what would become eastern Canada and New England teemed with cod and other species. The area, called the Georges Bank, was the most abundant fishing ground in the world.

Now, 500 years later, overfishing has reduced the number of fish to dangerously low levels. In response, Canada has closed the area to cod fishing and set strict limits on catches of other species.

When Canada took similar measures to protect the supply of herring in the 1970s, the fish eventually recovered. But experts say that some species today have been so depleted, they may never recover. The government also faces protests from Canadian fishermen. About 40,000 are now unemployed as a result of the fishing bans and loss of their fish supply.

SELF-EVALUATION

Were you able to read this section three times in 2:15?   YES   NO

What is the environmental problem in Canada?

_____

_____

What has the Canadian government done to solve the problem?

_____

_____

_____

_____

Continue reading the next section: Costa Rica

Reading Rate Goal: 175 wpm

Directions: Read the section on Costa Rica three times in 2:00.

Reading Comprehension Goal: What are the environmental problems in Costa Rica? What steps has the Costa Rican government taken to solve the problems? After reading this section, write your answers to these two questions then share your responses with a partner.

Costa Rica

This Central American country has one of the most ambitious programs in the world to preserve the ecological diversity of its rain forests. Much of the country has already been deforested, and soil erosion has been extensive. But a series of new environmental laws, together with the creation of parks and nature preserves that cover one-quarter of the country, are aimed at protecting Costa Rica's remaining forests.

There is also a major effort under way to identify and catalogue local species to prevent their extinction. The world's largest pharmaceutical company, Merck & Co., is helping to pay for the project in exchange for the right to study endangered plants within the preserve for possible new medicines.

SELF-EVALUATION

Were you able to read this section three times in 2:00?   YES   NO
What are the environmental problems in Costa Rica?

_____

_____

What steps has the Costa Rican government taken to solve the problems?

_____

_____

_____

_____

Continue reading the next section: Brazil

Reading Rate Goal: 195 wpm
Directions: Read the section on Brazil three times in 2:00.
Reading Comprehension Goal: What is the environmental problem in Brazil? What has the Brazilian government done to solve the problem? After reading this section, write your answers to these two questions then share your responses with a partner.

Brazil

Brazil is home to the world's largest rain forest, the Amazon. For decades, the government sought to colonize and develop the Amazon, bringing severe environmental devastation to the area and its people.

But in 1991, under pressure from environmentalists around the world, Brazil reversed course. It ended tax subsidies that had encouraged clearing of the Amazon rain forest, and agreed to a plan to finance new forest protection projects.

Cattle ranchers, miners, and settlers have protested the move and continue to raze the forests, although at a slower pace than before. The conflict escalated last year when miners killed a group of Amazon Indians in order to seize their land. The government vows it will protect the region's indigenous tribes, but questions remain as to its true level of commitment.

Threads

Save Natural Resources—By making products from recycled materials instead of virgin materials, we reduce the need to cut down trees, drill for oil, and dig for minerals.

Environmental Defense Fund, New York

SELF-EVALUATION

Were you able to read this section three times in 2:00?   YES   NO
What is the environmental problem in Brazil?

_____

_____

What has the Brazilian government done to solve the problem?

_____

_____

_____

_____

Continue reading the next section: Eastern Europe

Reading Rate Goal: 185 wpm
Directions: Read the section on Eastern Europe three times in 2:00.
Reading Comprehension Goal: What is the environmental problem in Eastern Europe? What have the governments in Eastern Europe done to solve the problem? After reading this section, write your answers to these two questions then share your responses with a partner.

Eastern Europe

The nations of Eastern Europe, including Poland, Hungary, and the Czech and Slovak Republics, are considered the most polluted of all the world's industrialized countries. Heavy metals from coal mining have tainted much of the area's waters. Rivers, land, and forests are so contaminated that many are now biologically dead.

In a special series of treaties, Eastern European countries and other nations, including the United States, have set up special funds for environmental cleanups and modernization of the region's power plants. In addition, Germany and the Czech Republic have signed a treaty to protect the Elbe River from further contamination. Experts say the treaty could serve as a model for protecting other rivers in the region, including the Oder and Danube.

SELF-EVALUATION

Were you able to read this section three times in 2:00?   YES   NO
What is the environmental problem in Eastern Europe?

_____

_____

Threads

Save energy—It usually takes less energy to make recycled products: recycled aluminum, for example, takes 95 percent less energy to make than new aluminum.

Environmental Defense Fund, New York

What have the governments in Eastern Europe done to solve the problem?

_____

_____

_____

_____

Continue reading the next section: Ghana

Reading Rate Goal: 185 wpm

Directions: Read the section on Ghana three times in 2:00.

Reading Comprehension Goal: What is the environmental problem in Ghana? What has the government in Ghana done to solve the problem? After reading this section, write your answers to these two questions then share your responses with a partner.

Ghana

Ghana's population has been growing by 3.2 percent a year. This explosive growth has led to the deforestation of much of the country, and the overuse of existing farmland. Forests have been cut down at the rate of 278 square miles a year.

In response, the government has urged local villages to create more communal farmland. It has sponsored the growing of cash crops such as cassava, maize, and cotton, and the planting of trees to regenerate desolate land. Observers say the program has succeeded in strengthening the country's agricultural base and bringing a new source of wealth to villagers. But it remains to be seen whether these measures will have enough impact to slow the rate of deforestation.

SELF-EVALUATION

Were you able to read this section three times in 2:00?   YES   NO

What is the environmental problem in Ghana?

_____

_____

What has the government in Ghana done to solve the problem?

_____

_____

_____

_____

Continue reading the next section: Indonesia

Reading Rate Goal: 175 wpm

Directions: Read the section on Indonesia three times in 2:30.

Reading Comprehension Goal: What is the environmental problem in Indonesia? What has the government in Indonesia done to solve the problem? After reading this section, write your answers to these two questions then share your responses with a partner.

Indonesia

Indonesians have traditionally favored large families, and their predominant religion, Islam, frowns on birth control. But with 188 million people, the country is now struggling to provide enough food, shelter, and jobs for its people. In recent years, the government has waged a massive ad campaign to encourage birth control, offering inducements such as free trips to Mecca, the birthplace of Islam in Saudi Arabia.

The government has succeeded in increasing contraceptive use from 10 percent of the population 20 years ago to 49 percent today. As a result, the average number of births has been cut from 5.6 children per woman to 3. The government hopes to reduce it to 2.1 children per woman by 2005. But with such a large population base, the country must still convert millions more to the idea of birth control if it is to reach its population targets.

SELF-EVALUATION

Were you able to read this section three times in 2:30?   YES   NO

What is the environmental problem in Indonesia?

_____

_____

_____

What has the government in Indonesia done to solve the problem?

_____

_____

_____

_____

Reading 1: Post-Reading Comprehension Check

THINK!

What have you learned about environmental awareness as a result of reading *One Step at a Time?*

Fill out the following grid listing the environmental problems and solutions from each of the countries you just read about.

COUNTRY/REGION	PROBLEM	SOLUTION
1. _____	_____	_____
2. _____	_____	_____
3. _____	_____	_____
4. _____	_____	_____
5. _____	_____	_____
6. _____	_____	_____

READING 2: RECYCLING BINS FRIVOLOUS

Pre-Reading Discussion

LEARNING STRATEGY

Personalizing: Sharing information with partners is a good way to get some idea of what to expect from a reading.

Discuss the following with a partner.

1. Do you currently recycle?
2. What do you recycle?
3. If you do not recycle, why don't you?
4. Is recycling done in your country? If so, what types of recycling are done? If not, why not?
5. Should you contribute money to help set up places to recycle materials?

IT WORKS!
Learning Strategy:
Setting a Goal
for Improved
Reading Rate

Set a reading rate goal for this passage? Record that goal here: _____

Reading Skill Improvement

READING RATE INSTRUCTION

Rate Buildup Reading. Try to read more in each 60-second period as you do four 60-second reading rate buildup segments. Don't just skim the material but read!

Threads

Things to recycle: newspaper, magazines, cardboard, paper, glass, aluminum.

Threads

Reduce the amount of waste that we generate. Reuse the products and packaging that we do create. Recycle the raw materials.

U.S. PIRG, Washington, D.C.

IT WORKS!
Learning Strategy:
Evaluating Your
Reading Rate

READING 2: RECYCLING BINS FRIVOLOUS

by Ohio University Post, Editorial

The university just spent $40,000 on recycling bins for administration buildings and residence hall rooms. Boy, that is a lot of pop cans and old newspapers. While it is admirable that the administration is environmentally aware and politically correct, the money could have
5 been spent more efficiently.

Buying bins for administration buildings is a good idea, but putting bins in dorm rooms is silly. How hard is it to walk downstairs to the recycling areas in each residence hall, usually placed near the dumpsters? On a campus where many people have to walk everywhere,
10 it does not seem that challenging.

If anything, the university could spend some of the money by giving students jobs. One or two students in every hall could have jobs recycling a single set of bins.

The university can certainly come up with something better to do
15 with $40,000 than spend it on unnecessary recycling bins. Here are some suggestions:

- Scholarships. A university can never give away too many scholarships, and scholarships would most certainly be a popular idea with students.
- Give it to a sports program to attract recruits—no, not in the form
20 of illegal cash payments. Buy some weights, some new uniforms, whatever it takes to have a winning sports program.
- Parking. This one could even be profitable. If the university built more parking lots, then it could charge more people to park.
- Buy more computers. Also, leave the labs open longer. Some people
25 think best after midnight, but the labs are closed then. And what about when you wake up at 3 a.m. and remember that paper that is due at 9 a.m.

OK, so $40,000 won't cover all of these ideas. But it could help some of them. And it just makes more sense to reward hard-working students
30 with scholarships than to reward lazy students with recycling bins so they can be environmentally responsible without getting out into the environment.

Evaluate your reading rate performance.

1. How many lines of text did you read the first time? Write the number here: _____
2. Multiply the number of lines you read the first one-minute segment by 10. Write the product here: _____ (This is approximately the number of words that you read the first minute.)
3. How many lines of text did you read the fourth time? Write the number here: _____
4. Multiply the number of lines you read the fourth one-minute segment by 10. Write the product here: _____ (This is approximately the number of words that you read the fourth minute.)
5. What was your reading rate goal? Write your goal here: _____
6. Compare the numbers in #2 and #4 above with your goal in #5. How well did you do in reaching your reading rate goal?

Reading 2: Post-Reading Comprehension Check

Remembering New Material: Writing down what you remember after reading is a good way to increase your comprehension.

Below, list the information that you remember reading in the passage *Recycling Bins Frivolous.* Do not refer back to the reading passage.

Discuss what you recall about the passage with a small group of students in the class. What information did all of you recall? What information did you recall that others did not? What information did others recall that you did not? As a group, discuss what you learned about the author's reasons for thinking that recycling bins are frivolous.

If your university spent $40,000 on recycling bins for the student dormitories, what would your reaction be? Do you think that this is a good way to spend that amount of money? Why or why not?

IT WORKS!
Learning Strategy:
Discussing What
You Have Read

_____

_____

_____

_____

_____

_____

_____

_____

_____

Threads

What's in trash?
37.5 percent paper,
17.9 percent yard waste,
7 percent glass,
8.5 percent metals,
8 percent plastic,
6.7 percent food,
14.4 percent other.

U.S. PIRG, Washington, D.C.

Now, compare your ideas with those of others in your class.

Forming Concepts: Predicting the content of the passage helps prepare you for your reading.

READING 3: TOO GREEN FOR THEIR OWN GOOD

Pre-Reading Discussion

Nations of the world can be grouped according to their degree of commitment to environmental issues. Five categories for grouping countries are: spectators, passive environmentalists, lip-service environmentalists, negotiators, and anxious experts.

What do you think these "titles" mean?

Match the following definitions with each of these group titles. Write the letter of the definition before the term it defines.

_____ **1.** spectators

_____ **2.** passive environmentalists

_____ **3.** lip-service environmentalists

_____ **4.** negotiators

_____ **5.** anxious experts

a. These are the "very worried" environmentalists who emphasize the role of business and accept personal responsibility.

b. These are the highly consumer-driven societies that profess awareness of and concern for environmental effects but adopt a largely superficial attitude about them.

c. These have a relatively low awareness of environmental problems, and when they do become aware, they blame their government.

d. These have serious concerns about their environment, but are passive in their response to it because of larger social problems.

e. These are countries that are aware of and concerned about environmental problems but take a cautious approach to them. They will use ecologically-friendly products but rarely focus on "greenness" as a goal.

Predict into which group each of the following 22 countries falls.

COUNTRIES	CATEGORIES				
	SPECTATORS	PASSIVE ENVIRONMENTALISTS	LIP-SERVICE ENVIRONMENTALISTS	NEGOTIATORS	ANXIOUS EXPERTS
Argentina	____	____	____	____	____
Australia	____	____	____	____	____
Belgium	____	____	____	____	____
Brazil	____	____	____	____	____
Canada	____	____	____	____	____
Chile	____	____	____	____	____
Columbia	____	____	____	____	____
France	____	____	____	____	____
Germany	____	____	____	____	____
Greece	____	____	____	____	____
India	____	____	____	____	____
Italy	____	____	____	____	____
Japan	____	____	____	____	____
Netherlands	____	____	____	____	____
New Zealand	____	____	____	____	____
Nigeria	____	____	____	____	____
Norway	____	____	____	____	____
South Africa	____	____	____	____	____
Spain	____	____	____	____	____
United Kingdom	____	____	____	____	____
United States	____	____	____	____	____
Uruguay	____	____	____	____	____

GOAL SETTING

Set a goal for the number of words-per-minute you want to reach while reading *Too Green for Their Own Good.* Record that goal here: _____

What is the reading comprehension goal? Record that goal here: _____

IT WORKS! Learning Strategy: Setting a Reading Rate Goal

READING 3: TOO GREEN FOR THEIR OWN GOOD

by Gary Levin

Awareness of the world's environmental problems has made a dramatic increase in recent years. This awareness is good as it helps all people focus on keeping our
5 environment clean and green. Wise use of the earth's resources is very important. However, this increase in awareness may cause anxiety and confusion among those exposed to an overabundance of
10 information. The amount of information about the environment continues to grow. With so much information it is often difficult for people to know what to do to have a positive influence on the environment. Also,
15 individuals often do not know how to help influence the governments of their countries to make changes which will protect the environment. This is the key finding of a new study from Research International,
20 which gathered information in 29 countries. The purpose of the research was to define how people from different cultures accept and react to environmental awareness.

Researchers found that in countries
25 where the environment is a hot topic, many citizens expressed concern but seemed helpless about how to cope with the issue. "The more you know, the less you know how to deal with it," said Simon Chadwick,
30 chairman and CEO of Research International. Mr. Chadwick's response was similar to the attitude expressed by many of the more than 900 respondents. An "overload" of information can be a difficult
35 thing to handle. What can individuals do with all the information available about the environment?

In some countries, "the more information that is given . . . the more
40 contradictory it seems, and the less people are able to translate that information into knowledge," Mr. Chadwick said. Feeding into the overload are businesses that have jumped on the environmental bandwagon.
45 Some of these businesses have poorly defined claims of environmental "friendliness." And most of these businesses are found in highly developed countries.

But countries divide up responsibility
50 for the environment differently: More heavily Roman Catholic countries depend on the government, while mostly Protestant countries say they take personal responsibility or assign it to individual
55 businesses to handle.

"As the public becomes more expert, there is a large amount at stake for businesses in terms of how they deal with it," Mr. Chadwick said.
60 Consumers are "looking for clarity of information that can lead people to make decisions," he said, "and they are looking for evidence of social and ethical behavior on the part of businesses being honest as well
65 as clear."

Companies that try to exploit interest in the environment without contributing to it themselves will be quickly recognized by environmentally aware citizens, Mr.
70 Chadwick said. "The more 'greenness' becomes a competitive weapon, the more a company that runs an environmental ad but does nothing about it will be shown up," he said.
75 Research International held discussion groups of eight to 10 environmentally aware citizens. The purpose of these discussion groups was to reveal the individual's perceptions about influences of food,
80 cosmetics and medical products, as well as natural or social phenomena, on the environment. In the U.S., a total of six discussion groups were conducted in Boston and San Francisco. The discussions yielded

insights that allowed researchers to divide the countries into five groups according to consumers' degree of environmental awareness and action:

- Spectators. Least developed, poorer countries, including India, Kenya, Nigeria, Brazil and Chile, have relatively low awareness of environmental problems, and when they do, they blame their governments. Manufacturers are rarely perceived negatively. Instead, researchers reported an "obsession" with imported products made elsewhere, perceived as luxury brands with higher quality standards. Consumers seek foods with fewer preservatives and better product labeling.

- Passive environmentalists. While similar to the spectators, residents of Colombia, South Africa, and to some extent Uruguay, have serious concerns about their environment, but are passive in their response to it because of larger social problems.

The common attitude is "I'm aware of it, I'm concerned about it but I cannot deal with it right now," Mr. Chadwick said. Residents are more interested in improving their social climate than they are in furthering environmental causes.

- Lip-service environmentalists. Highly consumer-driven societies, like many in Southern Europe, Australia and Argentina, profess awareness of and concern for environmental effects but adopt a largely superficial attitude about them. Citizens seem concerned about issues like recycling but place responsibility for environmental issues on their governments.

This group seems unwilling to trade convenience and disposability for a reduction in preservatives or other additives, but would buy products they consider safer if both price and performance were equal.

Manufacturers were almost entirely excused from responsibility for environmental problems.

- Negotiators. Consumers in countries like the U.K., France, Japan and New Zealand are aware of and concerned about environmental problems but take a cautious approach to them. They will use ecologically-friendly products "if the price and quality are the same and allow them to minimize guilt," Mr. Chadwick said. They rarely focus on "greenness" as a goal. Most of the time they place responsibility for their surroundings on businesses.

- Anxious experts. These are the "very worried" environmentalist living in Scandinavian countries, Germany, Canada and the U.S. (especially in California). They emphasize the role of businesses but also accept blame themselves for factors influencing their own health as well as the global environment.

"These people are almost off the edge where naturalness is concerned," Mr. Chadwick said. "The more old-fashioned the product, the more it can be proved to be natural, the more interested they are."

The primary restraint, he added, is higher prices, if the price gap is narrowed the sales of products perceived to be environmentally safer will increase.

People throughout the world are becoming more environmentally aware. Some of these individuals can be called "too green for their own good." By focusing on keeping the environment green these people need to learn how to work with their governments to also become more environmentally aware. As everyone works together in improving the environment the task will become easier and we can keep the earth's environment green.

ENDING TIME: _____ : _____
TOTAL TIME: _____
1000 WORDS ÷ _____ MIN = _____ WORDS/MIN

Record your reading rate on the rate chart in Appendix B.

Compare the placement below of the 22 countries into the five degrees of environmentalism with the placement you made before you read. How close were your predictions?

FIVE DEGREES OF ENVIRONMENTALISM

Spectators: Brazil, Chile, Nigeria
Passive Environmentalists: South Africa, Colombia, Uruguay
Lip-service Environmentalists: Spain, Italy, Australia, Greece, Argentina
Negotiators: France, Belgium, Japan, U.K., New Zealand
Anxious Experts: U.S., Canada, Germany, Netherlands, Norway

Reading 3: Post-Reading Comprehension Check

Without looking back at the passage *Too Green for Their Own Good,* complete the following comprehension statements/questions by circling the appropriate letter.

1. The primary purpose of the research on environmental awareness by Research International was to
   a. divide countries into categories on how environmentally aware their citizens are.
   b. look at how people from different countries use information about environmental awareness.
   c. provide additional information about environmental awareness to add to existing material.
   d. identify what businesses are doing to help promote environmental awareness in the world.

2. Many people say they are concerned about environmental awareness although they
   a. leave the responsibility to religion, government, or business.
   b. give only lip-service to the ideas and do not take real action.
   c. are more concerned about their own safety and nothing else.
   d. find it difficult to understand all the information about the issues.

3. Religion plays a key role in the way some countries
   a. distribute responsibility for environmental issues.
   b. deal with the social climate of environmental topics.
   c. give lip-service to citizens concerned with the environment.
   d. show more concern for old-fashioned products.

4. India, Kenya, Nigeria, Brazil, and Chile are classified as _____ on the five degrees of environmentalism.
   a. passive environmentalists
   b. anxious experts
   c. lip-service environmentalists
   d. spectators

5. Some businesses have the appearance of being environmentally aware but
    a. are more influenced by what their customers say.
    b. lack the support of the government.
    c. only do so to be part of the social movement.
    d. are really only passive environmentalists.

6. Paying lip service to environmental issues means that
    a. you believe in environmental matters but are not fully committed to them.
    b. you support government involvement to minimize feelings of guilt.
    c. the price for environmentally safe products is the same as other products.
    d. you emphasize the role of businesses but also accept some of the blame.

7. The United States, Canada, Germany, Netherlands, and Norway are classified as _____ on the five degrees of environmentalism.
    a. lip-service environmentalists
    b. anxious experts
    c. negotiators
    d. passive environmentalists

8. In the five degrees of environmentalism, Russia would probably be classified as
    a. spectators.
    b. lip-service environmentalists.
    c. negotiators.
    d. passive environmentalists.

9. What does the title, *Too Green for Their Own Good* mean?
    a. Spectators have serious concerns about the environment but are passive in their response.
    b. Religions take on far more responsibility for environmental awareness than they should.
    c. Environmentally aware people may be unable to bring about changes in some countries of the world.
    d. People need to work together to improve the earth's environment and to keep it green.

10. Keeping the earth's environment green is easier when
    a. citizens and governments are working together.
    b. the passive environmentalists do not conflict with the spectators.
    c. governments and businesses take the responsibility.
    d. churches combine efforts with government and business.

Total number of correct answers: _____ / 10

Record your reading comprehension score on the comprehension chart in Appendix C.

> **Threads**
>
> Save landfill space—
> When the materials that you recycle go into new products, they don't go into landfills or incinerators, so scarce landfill space is conserved.
>
> Environmental Defense Fund, New York

Record your reading rate on the reading graph in Appendix B. How does your reading rate on this passage compare with your rate on previous passages? Slower? Faster? The same?

Did you reach the reading rate goal you set before reading?

Each of the comprehension questions above can be classified into one of three reading comprehension categories:

IT WORKS!
Learning Strategy:
Self-Evaluating

- Understanding Main Ideas,
- Understanding Direct Statements, or
- Understanding Inferences.

Review your performance on each question and record your performance on the chart provided in Appendix B. How does your reading comprehension on this passage compare with the previous passages? Lower? Higher? The same?

Did you reach the reading comprehension goal you set before reading?

After checking your answers, review each one that you marked incorrectly and determine WHY you missed the question.

POST-READING EVALUATION

Respond in writing to the following questions, then discuss your answers with others in your class.

1. What have you learned from all the readings in this chapter on environmental awareness?

IT WORKS!
Learning Strategy:
Evaluating What
You Have Learned

_____

_____

_____

_____

_____

2. How has your knowledge changed as a result of these readings?

_____

_____

_____

_____

_____

_____

3. How has your attitude changed as a result of these readings?

_____
_____
_____
_____
_____

4. What can you do to show that you are more environmentally aware?

_____
_____
_____
_____
_____

5. Look back at the goals you set at the beginning of this chapter.
Which goals did you achieve?

_____
_____
_____

Forming Concepts: Reading graphs helps you visualize reading material.

Review your reading rate graph and reading comprehension graph in Appendices B and C.

Answer the following questions based on these graphs.

1. What do you learn about your reading rate as you *read* these graphs?

_____

_____

_____

2. Is the reading rate graph consistent from chapter to chapter or is there a difference among chapters?

_____

_____

_____

3. In which chapter did you have your highest reading rate?

_____

4. Why do you think you had your fastest reading rate in this chapter?

_____

_____

_____

5. In which chapter did you have your lowest reading rate?

_____

6. Why do you think you had your slowest reading rate in this chapter?

_____

_____

_____

7. What do you learn about your reading comprehension as you *read* these graphs?

_____

_____

8. Is the reading comprehension graph consistent from chapter to chapter or is there a difference among chapters?

_____

_____

9. In which chapter did you have your highest reading comprehension score?

_____

10. Why do you think you had your highest reading comprehension score in this chapter?

_____

_____

_____

11. In which chapter did you have your lowest reading comprehension score?

_____

12. Why do you think you had your lowest reading comprehension score in this chapter?

_____

_____

_____

13. Write a summary of what you learn about your own reading based on these graphs. Then share what you have learned with a partner.

_____

_____

_____

_____

_____

_____

_____

_____

_____

_____

_____

WHAT HAVE YOU LEARNED?

Think about the questionnaires you completed in Chapter 1. What have you learned about yourself? Has your knowledge of your learning style helped you while reading? Has knowledge of your reading strategy profile helped you while reading? Record your ideas and thoughts below.

IT WORKS!
Learning Strategy:
Self-Evaluating

_____

_____

_____

_____

_____

_____

_____

_____

Discuss with a partner what you have learned about yourself.

Optional Activity

Answer the questions from the Strategy Inventory for Language Learning and Style Analysis Survey again (completed in Chapter 1). Then compare your learning strategies profile and your learning styles profile now that you have completed all the chapters of *Real Contexts.*

What have you learned about yourself? Record your ideas and thoughts below.

_____

_____

_____

_____

_____

_____

Share the comparison profiles with a partner.

Appendices

READING LOG

Name: _____

Date	Reading Time	Reading Material	Comments
_____	_____	_____	_____
_____	_____	_____	_____
_____	_____	_____	_____
_____	_____	_____	_____
_____	_____	_____	_____
_____	_____	_____	_____
_____	_____	_____	_____
_____	_____	_____	_____
_____	_____	_____	_____
_____	_____	_____	_____
_____	_____	_____	_____
_____	_____	_____	_____
_____	_____	_____	_____
_____	_____	_____	_____
_____	_____	_____	_____
_____	_____	_____	_____
_____	_____	_____	_____
_____	_____	_____	_____
_____	_____	_____	_____
_____	_____	_____	_____
_____	_____	_____	_____
_____	_____	_____	_____
_____	_____	_____	_____
_____	_____	_____	_____
_____	_____	_____	_____
_____	_____	_____	_____

READING RATE										
TIME	**1**	**2**	**3**	**4**	**5**	**6**	**7**	**8**	**9**	**RATE**
1:00										1000
1:15										800
1:30										667
1:45										571
2:00										500
2:15										444
2:30										400
2:45										364
3:00										333
3:15										308
3:30										286
3:45										267
4:00										250
4:15										235
4:30										222
4:45										211
5:00										200
5:15										190
5:30										182
5:45										174
6:00										167
6:15										160
6:30										154
6:45										148
7:00										143
7:15										138
7:30										133
7:45										129
8:00										125
8:15										121
8:30										118
8:45										114
9:00										111
9:15										108
9:30										105
9:45										103
10:00										100

COMPREHENSION										
SCORE	1	2	3	4	5	6	7	8	9	%
10										100
9										90
8										80
7										70
6										60
5										50
4										40
3										30
2										20
1										10
0										0